PR
T5-AFS-398

1969

Date D

OCCASIONS · *A Volume of Essays upon Divers Subjects*

OCCASIONS

*A Volume of Essays on such Divers
Themes as Laughter and Cathedrals,
Town and Profanity, Gardens
and Bibliomania, Etc.*

By HOLBROOK JACKSON

Essay Index Reprint Series

 BOOKS FOR LIBRARIES PRESS
FREEPORT, NEW YORK

First Published 1922
Reprinted 1969

STANDARD BOOK NUMBER:
8369-1299-3

LIBRARY OF CONGRESS CATALOG CARD NUMBER:
77-93347

PRINTED IN THE UNITED STATES OF AMERICA

The CONTENTS

LANDMARKS

for

CECIL ROBERTS

*But the most pleasant of all out-
ward pastimes is that of* Are-
taeus, deambulatio per amoena
loca, *to make a petty progress, a
merry journey now and then with
some good companions, to visit
friends, see Cities, Castles,
Towns* . . . —ROBERT BURTON,
"The Anatomy of Melancholy"
(1651).

TOWN

SINCE it is man's privilege, and, I hope, delight, to sanctify that which he likes by praise, let me, liker of many things, sanctify in such time-hallowed manner that which upon most days, in most years, I like above all places. Let me praise Town. If you tell me it is unnecessary I shall agree with you, for has not mankind, from the days when he was a wild thing, perpetually cast halo upon halo upon the brows of his favourite ? Nevertheless, it is rarely too late to praise what is good, especially when there exist those who are churlish enough to belittle Town in the light of Country. Country, forsooth ! What service hath it, save to minister to the needs of Town ! Let us pass on.

Neither do I imagine that I am unique in my advocacy even as a writer. Others—a good company, mark you—have forestalled and forestalled me. What then ? There is small virtue in being different in our day : it is the fashion. So let me also write of Town after my own manner, and with such reverence as befits so great a subject and so unworthy a pen.

Not, let me hasten to add, of any town, though to be sure half a town is better than no town at all—even though you own it not, the which, I am told, generally happens. When I write of Town I write of Town, not of this town or that town, not of London or Paris, neither of Venice nor Oxford, nor Florence, nor Bath, nor Bruges, nor Rome; nor yet write I of Bagdad or Babylon, Damascus or Samarkand: good towns all, but I write not of them. I write of Town. I celebrate all of these master cities in the soul of each—domed or towered or turreted, roofed in red or grey or purple, walled or free, filled with trees or threaded by river or canal, piercing heaven with spire or striking it with minaret, it is all of these in the final expression of man's creativeness—his *chef-d'œuvre*—Town.

Town is the place wherein during your sanest moments, the place, passing all places, wherein you would spend your time from choice, and to be happy in that choice you must be a devout attendant on Her Ladyship the Country. You must be equal to making a sonnet to her russet eyebrows ; capable, when she greets your impending departure with an April storm, of holding her soft hand, as it were, and gazing deep, deep into her peerless green eyes with a lover's assurance and undying faithfulness ; and you must believe it is true though you know it is not. For every proper man flirts with the Country, and weds Town.

There are those who, knowing this, are woebegone. Heed them not—they are the species before last. They have not reached our stage. How they cry with voices meet for moorside or paddock—" Back to the Land ! " Let them cry and let them go, say I. Back to Town for me and mine. And as for Country, the hussy, and her propaganding yokels, let her keep her place and them their noise. Go to ! Are there no such things as week-ends ! And what more can she want, pray ? But let us have patience ; let us not vex ourselves in so lost a cause. Indeed, are not all causes lost causes, and Town, having no need of advocacy, victorious ? When man left Eden he went to Town : and there he has remained, faithful to the friendly bricks and stones he has piled about him in protecting glories of artifice.

13

Hearken to the sound of it—*Town—Town !*
The very word is melody—nay, harmony, a bell-
glad word for a multitudinous thing.

I hear all the music of artifice in it—the magic
of made things. It sings to me of all the æons that
matter—the long ages of man. It is the *motif* of
the greatest of all tone-poems, and comprises—
homes and churches : houses of man and God—
streets that are rivers of traffic, and quiet streets
like lakes ; and lagoon-like avenues and pond-like
closes where houses grow more beautifully than
trees, and grass is teased out of all natural
ungainliness, until it recalls the soft rich velvets
made by man, and the cool green lakes for fays
that never were. And fabrics in stone : foliated,
and splintered into spires and pinnacles. Massed
masonry, heaped and spacious against the changing
sky. And courts and alleys, and the broad, tireless
streets and the endless terraces ; and light, light
everywhere, playing a myriad pranks out of sheer
joy in such an eternal maze. Glancing over building and roadway, striking colour out of grey and
white and drab, as fire is struck from flint and
steel ; pouring into squares and filling them as
fountain-basins are filled with silver water or

14

goblets with golden wine ; hurling javelins of fire into dark alleyways or dim quadrangles—laughing, lilting, splashing—scattering stars and diadems as a king scatters honours upon those who serve him ; setting a crown of gold upon Town and a nimbus of light above the crown. . . .

So is Town glorified.

And in the great harmony there are more familiar strains—intimate tunes for delight, and discords for contrast. Taverns and resting-places, parks and gardens, and silent places of the dead ; storehouses of beauty and knowledge and merchandise ; workshops, and palaces of pleasure and places of prayer and praise. And innumerable odd places, nooks and corners, and surprising *culs-de-sac*. Oh, the crannies and canyons, and precipitous walls, the spires and towers vaunting sound, and the shafts waving smoke and steam, and the machines and the vehicles and the horses, and ever and ever the myriad changeful stream of mankind, stirring, quick and slow, talking, laughing, shouting, singing, weeping, silent, amid the massy art-work of their creating, merged in the ordered chaos sprung from their needs and their follies, their activities and their indolence !

Such is Town, and more than that. Town is far more than that. Town even contains the Country. There are parks. There are gardens. Town does not need to bring Country to her doors : that is the parvenu ambition of the suburbs—*aquila non capit muscas*. Besides, it is not good that a park should ape nature—a park should aspire to the condition of landscape before Turner, of gardens before Paxton. One should never forget that a park is an act of man and that man has always aspired to the condition of convention. In the country he cannot be conventional, for as soon as he begins to be so a town springs up around him and he is no longer in the country. It is his whim to tell and retell himself that one day he may return to his native state : but he never does, and he never will. Country sentiment always synchronizes with town growth. For every stone and iron *motif* added to the tone-poem of Town a nature poet comes to life, seeking to remind man always of the Eden he has missed, recalling him always to that state of adoration for natural things which all true townsmen believe in their hearts to be the true faith, so true that it always confirms them in their love of Town.

Surely it is an article of grace in such matters that you cannot know Town is Heaven until you believe Country is. But your true townsman is no refugee fled from the tyranny of country dullness. Only the yokel flies from rural things. Townsmen built Town, and Town returned the compliment. He loves the country, and none the less because he prefers on most occasions to meet her *via* some poem or pastoral picture. And when he desires nearer acquaintance of her, which he does occasionally, he goes to her in person, and, if good weather be in attendance, is enraptured by her grace, strengthened by her purity, inspired by her lust—and all the more so because he can get away from her by the next train.

So is Town justified again and again in a thousand ways, and mainly for one reason—but reasons are for the unreasonable ; they prove only what you want them to prove, be it good or bad. Town is beyond such cheap subterfuges. " The axis of the earth sticks out visibly through the centre of each and every Town." That is not a reason ; the author of those words, Oliver Wendell Holmes, merely stated a fact.

INTERIOR: MILAN CATHEDRAL

IT is difficult to approach such a monument of human ingenuity as the Cathedral of Milan without bookishly-acquired prepossessions. As I walked across the Piazza, Ibsen's words came into my mind : " The man who conceived that Cathedral could have made moons in his spare time and thrown them into space." I found my brain repeating these words as the vast grey mass of clustered and regimented spires and pinnacles, grey and gracious in the November mist, became more clearly defined. Milan as a spectacle, a spectacle in stone, a triumph of architecture, of intricate grace, stands alone among religious buildings, as it stood before me there, lonely in the mist of a November afternoon.

But the impression of grace which is gained from an exterior view changes into something dimly heavy and sinister once you pass within. Inside it is nearly dark. It is like entering a cave. You feel the vastness of the place in spite of the darkness, as though you had entered a hollow mountain ; you half expect bats to flutter by. The carvings and traceries appear and disappear fantastically in the gloom. The only light comes from the clusters of votive candles about little distant altars. They look like jewels and give the same sort of light, or rather keep a similar sort of light to themselves, begrudging to diffuse it. The light from the coloured windows is negligible. The windows are translucent tapestries hung upon invisible walls.

You feel your way, and feel very little also beside the great columns which spring apparently from nowhere to lose themselves in dark vaults among arabesques in dim grey stone. It is a ghostly realm. You are conscious of people moving about, and almost stumble over a woman at prayer. She kneels on the stone pavement looking small and helpless, a mere speck of blacker blackness in the gloom. There is a faint smell of incense, dim and furtive as the light : the ghostly survival of centuries of swinging censers. The people are ghosts, and the sculpture and the wrought iron ; the whole Cathedral is a ghost ; it is discarnate—dead, yet alive. It has a sinister beauty, the beauty of frustrate decaying and desolate things. You have a feeling of uncleanness as you immerse yourself in it and resolve not to be contaminated. It is like walking through an area infected by some morbidly fascinating disease, but with the consciousness that you will escape contagion.

A light escapes through a *grille* in the pavement surrounded by an iron railing. We are curious, and peep over the railings, and through the *grille* we see a crypt-like place with red-covered chairs and a priest gliding about and one or two people. But we cannot see well, as half the *grille* is covered with a cloth as if it were not desirable that the casual onlooker should see more. It adds to the ghostliness. So we pass away and are drawn towards a little shrine where there are many women worshippers and tiers of candles dimly burning with slowly moving flames. The women look as if they were frightened of something, as if something might happen, something that they desire but which none the less may not be all they desire. Living souls afraid of life and not quite certain of the advantages of death.

The darkness is now more familiar. We have merged into it and become for the moment a part of its dim life. We can see things. Gated doors, shrines, effigies, tables, more people ; and a little fat man with a rubicund face, watery, red-rimmed eyes, and black skull-cap on the back of his head like a sticking-plaster, comes to us, a very Caliban of the cavern, and in Anglo-Franco-Italian asks us whether we would like to see the relics. We would. He then leads us towards a heavy door, which he opens, and we pass into a room in charge of a pleasant-looking priest who reverently opens the doors of cupboards which are hung round the walls, revealing rows of life-sized silver effigies of popes and cardinals ; crucifixes and candelabra, coronets and mitres, and other symbols of religious pomp, jewelled and carven with fantastic designs of the most delicate and beautiful craftsmanship. He explains these treasures to us in a soft voice, and is obviously appreciative of our appreciation. He tells us that this silver statue was made by Michael Angelo, and that that rich bauble was copied from a masterpiece of Cellini. We admire the noble craftsmanship, but feel that it has nothing to do with the modern world : it is part of the paraphernalia of the ghostly realm we had entered, the bauble of some dead god.

We pass out again to the dim vastness of the Cathedral, where our moon-calf is waiting for us : a most attentive monster. He makes mysterious gestures, and his little red eyes almost sparkle as he leads us to a gate opening upon descending steps, and without a word, as if he were conferring upon us some inestimable privilege, he hands us over to the charge of another priestly figure, this time a sinister thing in a black cassock. It has a hushed voice which speaks English, a crooked nose too large for the face, goat's lips, and watery grey eyes. It is obviously one of Edgar Allan Poe's creatures come to life. We follow it down the steps and find ourselves in a small, well-lighted chamber, below the *grille* which had earlier excited our curiosity. We look up and see curious faces peering down as we had done. The room is irregular in shape with a groined and decorated stone roof, the walls are panelled in faded red brocade and tarnished silver. Facing the door is what looks like an altar, and below it a small narrow table covered with a red cloth. It is not an altar ; it is the sarcophagus of a saint : *San Carlo Padrone di Milano*. We admire, under guidance of the sinister priest, the superb workmanship of the silver tomb, and at an appropriate moment, gauged with the nicety of experience, the priest tells us that the dead saint lies within, and that for the small charge of five *lire* each we may have the privilege of gazing upon him. It is obviously an opportunity not to be missed. To see a real saint, though dead, for five *lire* with the exchange at 96·60 is a bargain. We agree to the proposal. The priest becomes theatrically impressive. He invests himself in a short white surplice taken from a box near by and begins to turn a handle. We half expect that some sort of music will be the result, but this proves only to be a profane reaction from memories of the familiar Italian music of the streets of England. The handle operates no mechanical keyboard—it serves a more novel purpose. As the priest winds, the silver panelled front of the sarcophagus moves and gradually glides down until it disappears, and a silver coffin, panelled in crystal, is revealed. There is the same magnificence of craftsmanship in all this flamboyant metal. Through the panels of bevelled rock-crystal we see the form of the dead Saint Charles, Cardinal of Rome, Archbishop of Milan, in all its costly vestments, white and red and gold, crozier of gold, mitre of gold, and holy ring on his white-gloved hand, as he lived three hundred years ago. Our priest lights the stump of a candle and moves it about before the corpse to make clearer the principal objects of interest: the ring, the crozier, and hanging above the face of the saint who has been dead for three hundred years, hanging close to the face of death—brown with decay, the bones showing through the broken parchment which was once flesh, and a glimpse of teeth through the decaying lips—hanging above the face of the saint who should have been buried three hundred years ago, is the most delicately beautiful jewelled coronet as ever came from the workshop of genius. The priest does well to add to its brightness the light of his little votive candle stump, for it is the work of Benvenuto Cellini himself.

The candle is then extinguished and the handle turned and the coffin closed in again. The tragedy is ended! We pay the guardian of Saint Charles and ascend once more into the dim Cathedral, where we are greeted by Caliban. We try to tip him and depart, but he has further services to offer and is not to be lightly shaken off.

Here is a great candelabrum, curiously wrought in iron with many a sacred and holy figure ; and he lights a match and takes us to a nearer view. This is the Holy Virgin, and that Abraham offering up his son Isaac, and this—and our moon-calf leers confidentially—and this—and he whispers words which convey obscene promises, pointing to obscure sculptures which presumably fulfil them. *Regardez !* We regard, but have to take the obscenity for granted: it is not obvious to our eyes—perhaps we are not Latin enough. Here again, persists Caliban, is the statue of a saint who was flayed alive—and in proof thereof he carries over his shoulder his own skin, displaying his quivering nerves and muscles as a warning to the faithful. . . .

*   *   *   *   *

We force a tip into the hand of Caliban and depart through the nearest door into the light of day on a wave of *grazie!*

A PORTRAIT OF MARSEILLES

Sun-baked and splashed with the faded colours of the East, Marseilles crowds her space of earth ; hot and huddled she is, like the corner of an overwrought farmyard in some sequestered part of a great domain. She catches the sunlight all day long, and in the darkness of the night, when *La Cannebière* is inhabited solely by the shadows of tall buildings and electric standards, it is but a laggard breeze that comes up from the Mediterranean. This gateway to the East and to the hot South seems to slumber rather than to wake. There is not, however, sufficient sun for the complete somnolence of the real East, but too much to awaken the quick step of the cities of the North. No one seems to hurry—life here is a perpetual stroll. Yet the streets are dense with the media of life ; they are packed more fully than those of any other European city I know— men, women, children, carts, electric cars, fiacres, and even taxis, these last looking ancient and battered, verging on the prehistoric ; and in and

26

out of the throng slouch and slink dogs—sleek and mangy dogs, big and little dogs, dogs with shaggy coats and dogs shaven and shorn like the poodles of the *Avenue des Champs Élysées,* and grey, naked sand terriers from Algeria, forming a kind of cement, a loose and flowing cement, to the ever-moving leisurely throng.

Doubtless, great industry has called Marseilles into being. There are evidences of it everywhere. Strange monstrous two-wheeled carts, blue painted and faded, loaded with bales and sacks of merchandise, mingled with the traffic, and at the bottom of the long streets converging on the port are forests of masts and the smoke-stacks of the merchantmen of many nations. But no one seems to make a fuss about it ; they take their commerce in Marseilles like a regiment standing at ease, because the whole city is lapped in hot sunlight and a perpetual state of slightly disturbed indolence seems to be natural. The people move from ship to quayside, from quayside to warehouse, from office to office, from house to house, from *café* to *café,* as if to-morrow would do. . . . Sitting at one of the little round tables on the *terrasse* of any of the many *cafés* of *La Cannebière* is like sitting and watching the movements of a very easy-going river.

*   *   *   *   *

Marseilles is a harmony in grey and drab, splashed with red and green and blue. But the reds and greens and blues are not the predominant colours ; they but serve to accentuate the over-whelming greyness and drabness of the place. Still, the grey of Marseilles is not the beaten-silver grey of London ; it is more like the iridescent grey of Paris, but different ; it is a grey that flirts with yellow, that leaps surprisingly into mottled bunches of colour with the movements of the sun. The colour of Marseilles changes like the colours in a kaleidoscope, but without the definite prismatic lines of the patterns made by that instrument. It is all vague, blurred, like the palette of a painter who works in low tones and astonishes you with their brilliance. It is a monotony that is never monotonous. Whilst looking at it your mind involuntarily searches round for fitting phrases in which to describe it, and musical terms suggest themselves most readily. You call it, to yourself, a harmony—a harmony in grey and gold, a harmony in drab and red, and so forth—and you feel that you are wrong every time, for the colour of Marseilles cannot be expressed in words. When a street is a canyon of precipitous ochre surfaces, broken by rows and rows of faded green and red and blue window shutters, from between which protrude poles bearing domestic banners representing the day's washing, and when one side lies in sombre shadow, and the other in vivid light, you realize that you are face to face with something beyond the art of the pen. Marseilles is a Picasso.

*   *   *   *   *

You do not go to Marseilles to see things—that is, if you are wise—and in truth there is very little to see, if you did. The only sight in Marseilles is Marseilles. *Notre Dame de la Garde*, to be sure, crowns one of her enfolding hills, and you may reach it, I believe, by a funicular railway, but I never verified that. And on the quayside, looking out over merchandise and mastheads, tower the domes of *La Cathédrale ;* and in from the harbour at the top of one of the hilly streets stands the ornate *Arc de Triomphe de la Porte d'Aix.* These are the specialities of the guide-book, but if you pay much attention to them you will miss Mar-

seilles. I know no place which rewards the hunter
of scenery and sights less than Marseilles ; she
offers an insidious rebuke to all such seekers after
novelty. I believe she has a catlike jealousy of such
seeking, because it draws you away from herself.
She is like a woman who claims your undivided
attention—and generally gets it, like the clever
woman she is, by never seeming to desire it. You
just take things easily, you take your ease at your
café, and, adopting her indolence, watch her lazily
through cigarette smoke ; she responds to such
quiet observation ; it pleases her, maybe it flatters
her, though that would be the last thing you would
imagine her to admit. Yes, I am quite sure she
likes to be watched thus, dreamily through
cigarette smoke and over the fragrance of a
café-filtre, with the dirty white awning, crudely
embroidered in red, flapping just above you.
I know she likes such observation, for in this wise
she came to me.

*   *   *   *   *

Down by the harbour beside the great basin of
the *Vieux Port* is the heart of her. There lie the
ships under the eye of *Notre Dame de la Garde ;*
only nothing but their proximity to the towering

30

drab houses of the quays makes them remarkable ; they are just the sort of ships that you see at Liverpool, or New York, or Hull, for the ship of to-day is the same all the world over, as befits such international machines. But here and there, in a little cluster, at the *bottok* of *La Cannebière*, for instance, there are indications of a difference in some of the rigging—a marked difference, for the man from the North. Looking at this little different cluster, as I did, and wondering what the difference might be, you feel that you are in the presence, perhaps for the first time in your life, as it was with me, of a genuinely foreign thing, for nothing in Europe is really foreign—we are all Europeans ; the foreign thing is the *lateen* sail, the sail of the East. Watching the blue-grey water of the harbour one day and the shadows of the many masts, zigzagging into unclear depths, I saw before me the serried masts of many little boats, with their sails reefed and yard-arms hanging diagonally from short masts; and, as I noted the Eastern grace of the spars, one of the boats moved out from the rest, and the *lateen*, a brown, heart-shaped sheet of canvas, was spread to the breeze, and a couple of tan-faced men, one in a blue and the other in a white blouse, steered her course ; and I saw her sail dreamily, indolently, but surely out towards *Notre Dame de la Garde*, until she was lost to sight ; and my mind's eye followed her into the Mediterranean beyond the *Ratonneau* and *Château d'If*, beyond the *Polègues*, until she spoke shores where the date-palms grow. The port of Marseilles may mean many things, to many people, but for me the great French port is nothing more than that little brown heart-shaped sail that went, in my mind's eye, to meet the East.

* * * * *

Idling round Marseilles, with as little object as possible, you are rewarded with many finds. You just drift ; and as you drift you find yourself in strange places. Suddenly out of a street like a *crevasse* you find yourself in a little square, which, although an organic part of the tangle of Marseilles, is like a new and tiny independent town ; it may have even a church of its own, and always many taverns. There are trees with dusty, grey-green trunks and leaves that seem faded even in springtime, casting freckled and fluttering shadows over the uneven roadways ; and underneath the trees, at the side of the road, beside a huge, oblong stone trough, kneel a group of women and children,

32

wringing and hammering the domestic linen, salving it with soap, and sousing it with dirty water, as though life held nothing else for them and never even spared them time to give themselves a share of the cleanliness they were creating. At a rickety table, outside a little dram shop, loll two men, sipping *cognac*, and at the doors of shop and house loll also men ; a basket-maker sits before the door of a cellar plying his ancient craft; and where the square sprawls into a street, a troupe of blind musicians twang lazy melodies from the souls of worn guitars. Such things happen in Marseilles, or you may stroll up and down the broad *Allées de Meilhan*, where stately trees cast darker shadows over a large and curious throng of promenaders, who seem neither to be promenading nor going about their masters' business. They are just strolling, a part of the endless stroll which is Marseilles. Your steps may eventually take you into the Italian quarter, wherein there are still more streets like canyons, and an air of garlic ; and once more you are in another city. You have crossed the frontier of France without leaving that fair and pleasant land; you are in Italy. Even the shops have changed, and the grocers seem to sell nothing but macaroni.

It is very dirty and very odorous, and very noisome, and there are tawny people, and golden-brown children tumbling in the gutters, and everywhere the good folk seem to be eating ; every other house seems to have a *restaurant* on the ground floor, and every *restaurant* throws its chairs and tables on to the pavement so that its clients may dine in whatever air may peradventure worm its way into the recesses of the Italian quarter. And while you eat, or while they eat, for you do not somehow eat here, dark Italian boys play light melodies on the accordion. I will not speak of the fusty old churches into which your feet may lead you, where good market folk go to pray and beggars invoke your pity in the name of Our Lady, for there will be no end to the tale. But no matter where feet or whim may guide you, your ultimate destiny is ever *La Cannebière,* that ample artery through which the lifeblood of Marseilles streams continuously. There you may join in the stroll, or rest endlessly at small round tables under white awnings, broidered over with their proprietors' names in flaming red, watching Marseilles through cigarette smoke ; or, if it be the appointed hour, over the fragrance of *bouillabaisse* and a flagon of Chianti.

34

A TOWN FOR SALE

I ONCE knew a man who rarely travelled far from his base : a not excessively attractive northern town. When I put it to him that an occasional change of scene might fire his genius (he was a painter) with new energy (he was getting slack), he laughed me off my admonitory perch. It appeared that he did travel ; went far and wide by what he termed the Imaginative Express. The process was simple, cheap (he was poor), and, for him, effective. You simply bought or borrowed or—a month after publication—begged a Bradshaw, booked a seat in your best easy chair, put on your most intimate pipe, opened the entrancing volume at any page, set off mentally from the first station that took your fancy, stared out of the window of your mind's eye, until you reached . . . well you generally reached Utopia or Eldorado, for the Imaginative Express would appear to be a little irresponsible and occasionally erratic. As often as not, starting from, say, Wigan, it would rattle uneasily over the smoke-charred mosses of South Lancashire, where chemical engineering has not yet learnt that cleanliness is next to godliness, and after a little while pull up suddenly at Dreamton-in-the-Vale, and the excursionist detrained among larches and silver birches and lush grass bathed in that wizard sunlight which only Corot knew. At least, so my painter told me, and I was ready to believe, for I also have adventured in the realm of fancy. I believe in Magic Carpets.

Mine does not transport me into familiar or unfamiliar regions of earth or heaven : it makes me rich—sitting thereon, enchaired of course, I buy what I want (not what I *need*, mark you, that would be too purposeful and not such fun). My wants, I find, are many and curious, but the most persistent and magnificent is for property which I know quite well I do not need, and which would in all chances be a nuisance to me did I awake and find my dream come true. But that is an inconsiderable consideration—my dreams are of such a quality, and so well stocked with park-set paradises and Tudor farmhouses, that I could not hope for their materialization. So much then for that, which when you come to think of it is an advantage, for to get all you want is much easier than to want all you get, as Alice might have observed to the Mad Hatter. Therefore, let us to the method of my madness. It is as simple as the Imaginative Express, and might without exaggeration be called the Wizard Estate Agent. All you have to do is to buy one of those fat weekly papers without which no country house is complete, and wherein are set forth delectably and luxuriously " desirable residences for sale." You play at buying them, but only those that inspire you with the exalted feeling that you cannot possibly live happily in any imaginable future unless your nice personality is set like a jewel or framed like a masterpiece in such or such a house on that or that demesne. It may be but a cottage (" converted "—O word of desecration and utility), " quite a miniature affair, hung about with trellised vine," or some Elizabethan grange, enriched by time, unspoilt by the rich, planted amid rose-gardens, rose-like itself, and barricaded against the world by ten thousand timbered acres, with a pond of ancient roach, " reputed to have been fed by Queen Elizabeth when she visited the place in 1589," a herd of deer, a trout stream

37

("well stocked"), stables, paddocks, walled garden, tennis-courts, and—be it not forgotten— "garage for five cars, six bathrooms, H. and C., and central heating." . . . You, in brief, turn your page and take your choice, and if upon waking you find yourself still in the faded hierarchy of your household gods, you will worship them all the more—for you have had great possessions without letting them have you.

Thus have I been a lord of acres, and I am well pleased. For some time now I have thought that my Wizard Estate Agent could offer me nothing new. He would seem to have rung the changes of real estate until variety sought relief in monotony and monotony itself was about to dissolve into unpretentiousness. I have not grumbled—there was no occasion ; not even during the dark days of August 1914, when estate agents thought no one would ever again desire " desirable properties." In those days I tasted all the anguish of seeing my dream-properties destroyed in catastrophic bombardments stretching from shore to shore of this dear England of ours, and then waking just sufficiently to find it was only a dream, and dreaming off again into happy possession. But, a few

38

days ago, I reached the zenith of my dreamland
speculations, not in the pages of my usual " house
and property guide," where the pictures are, but
among the sedate leaves of the *Spectator*, and here
it is :

By direction of the Right Honourable LORD STALBRIDGE
FOR SALE BY AUCTION
THE HISTORICAL TOWN OF
SHAFTESBURY
DORSET
800ft above Sea Level

The Town of SHAFTESBURY, with a rent roll of about
£4,900, is to be OFFERED by AUCTION in one Lot in the
early Autumn.

The Town occupies a lovely situation, and has great possi-
bilities as a health resort. The properties comprise Private
Houses, Banks, Post Office and principal Shops, Business
Premises ; the leading Hotels and Licensed Premises ; the
Cattle Market ; Ground Rents ; numerous Cottages, fine
Building Sites, &c. 800ft. above Sea Level, with magnificent
views.

Auctioneers : Messrs. KNIGHT, FRANK & RUTLEY,
20 HANOVER SQUARE, W.1.

A town for sale ! What a chance for the
dreamer—and the profiteer. But I lost no chances.
Without leave of the Right Honourable and noble
owner, or his more famous auctioneers—I made
my bid, and Shaftesbury was mine ! How splen-

39

didly I left it alone to dream of its founder,
Rudhudibras, and of Alfred who made his
daughter its first Abbess, of Dunstan who laid
St. Edward's body there, and of Canute who went
there to die. I was not tempted to avail myself
of the possibility of translating it into a " health
resort," I cast no covetous eye upon its " fine
Building Sites " : Shaftesbury was none the worse
for my bidding. And now my escapade is over—
the dream unrealized. Shaftesbury is really for
sale " in the early Autumn." It is no dream, but
cold fact. A town for sale—an old English town
—one of those masterpieces of the English genius
which are among the wonders—more than the
wonders, the delights of the world. One reads of
Charles the Second's sale of Dunkirk with
indifference. Dunkirk was a French town, and it
merely reverted to its rightful owners. Even the
sale of Covent Garden a few years ago left me cold,
save for passing wonderment that anyone could
possess so vast a sum as its purchase price : and
Covent Garden is something of a town lost in the
maze of London, with its own history and
personalities, church and theatre, clubs and
taverns. But the very fact that it has allowed itself

to get lost in London is a bulwark against sentiment when owners change. A town is different;
an old English town is unique—it is a part of
England—a living, breathing part of England,
with a reality of its own and a soul of its own,
wherein Englishfolk, who have made it what it is,
have dwelt for generations, family succeeding
family in those long chains of relationship unknown to the great cities, especially London,
where families are said to die out in three generations. An old English town for sale—why, it is
like dealing in flesh and blood. I wonder what the
people of Shaftesbury think about it. There is no
mention of them—only the rent they pay. Presumably they are going to be thrown in with the
houses, shops, banks, and hotels . . . they are
part of the " lot " to be " Offered by Auction "
when the leaves begin to fall from their neighbour-
ing trees and the swallows hold conferences about
their pending evacuation of English skies. They
are part of the speculation, the working material of
perhaps the " health resort " into which their
" historical " town may be translated. I have a
presentiment that somebody is going to " put a
hustle on " Shaftesbury. . . . Shaftesbury's most

exciting page of history is in the immediate future : the quaint old English town is " in the market." . . .

Who'll buy ! Who'll buy ! *Now, gentlemen, any advance upon* . . . But no, let us ring down the curtain. Good-bye, little Shaftesbury—thy peril is greater than I can bear.

PREJUDICES

for

RALPH HODGSON

However far some men may have gone in the science of impartiality, I am persuaded that there is not one of them but would be surprised if he could be shown how much farther he might go.— FULKE GREVILLE, " Maxims, Characters and Reflections " (1757).

THE PATHOS OF PROFANITY

"YOUR conversation this evening, Lord Illingworth, has been most immoral, but very interesting all the same." Whenever the remark is made by Mrs. Allenby in *A Woman of No Importance* something like a thrill of naughty appreciation passes through the theatre. So it is with profanity in life and letters. We are shocked —it is proper to be shocked. We are amused—it is necessary to be amused. If we were not shocked by others, how should we measure our own virtue ? But profanity needs no defence, profanity is the homage paid by disillusion to faith. It is more attractive than faith because faith carries no surprises. It is kinder than faith because faith is proud and confident. Above all, profanity bears with it the pathos of eternal rejection. Faith, reverence, the virtues, have hope—verily, they shall have their reward ; but, despised and rejected of men, profanity walketh alone without hope or comfort in the future, staking all passionately in the present. Profanity, like virtue, is its own reward.

We should be grateful to the profane, even when we condemn them, for where would some of us be if we had no one or nothing to blame ? "Voltaire," said Benjamin Jowett, himself not immune from academic profanities, " Voltaire has done more good than all Fathers of the Church put together." Was the Master of Balliol referring to Voltaire's most provocative piece of irony : " If there were no God it would have been necessary to invent Him," which only the hypersensitive would call profane, or to the profanely piquant half-truth : " God created man in His own image —and man has returned the compliment " ? Perhaps Jowett had in mind the former Voltairian phrase, which is more in accord with his own advice to an undergraduate of Balliol who had informed him that he could find no accurate reason for God's existence—" I cannot see any signs of Him in Nature, and when I look into my own heart He is not there." " You must either find Him by to-morrow morning," said Jowett, " or leave the college." To be ordered to find God overnight by one who had constantly to buttress his own belief by dialectics, and in the end hoped for the best rather than believed in it, is so ironic as to be a piece of profanity itself, despite orthodox intention.

But profanity is not confined to religious matters. Porson's favourite profanity was to " damn the nature of things "—which does not err on the side of exclusiveness. Secular profanity is presumably any blasphemy against the moral code or convention of time or place. It is not profane, for instance, to sing, as Rudyard Kipling does, that

The wildest dreams of Kew are the facts of Khatmandhu,
And the crimes of Clapham chaste in Martaban,

because you are merely stating fact ; but, if you are, say, a patrician in danger of losing your means of subsistence through revolution, it would be profane of you to say, as that most charming of English lady letter writers, Miss Emily Eden, asserts Lord Alvanley said during the troubles of the eighteen-thirties, that in such circumstances you would " keep a disorderly house and make Glengall your head waiter."

Profanity is an inevitable and, perhaps, necessary reaction from all accepted views. It usually admits a protest, but is not inherently purposeful,

47

still less propagandist. Profanity may spring from outraged reverence or allegiance ; from suffering or sorrow too hard to bear. It is difficult for us to see the tragedy through the not always unpleasant mists of theology without losing our sense of reality, but when we do so we feel the underlying reverence of the story of the old peasant woman who, upon hearing for the first time a full account of the Crucifixion, expressed the shattering wish that, " since it all happened so long ago, please God it wasn't true."

But if profanity is sometimes secular, it is generally a reaction from godlike pretensions. *Lèse-majesté* is only remembered when a king peacocks himself with godlike attributes. The last of the divine-right kings was William Hohenzollern, and *lèse-majesté* was last heard of in Germany. It even awoke humour in the German. Two citizens of Hanover were discussing the Emperor, and a policeman overheard one use the word " fool " and proceeded to make an arrest. The good citizens protested that they were discussing the Czar of Russia. " Tell that story to the Marines," said the policeman, in effect, " you must have meant the Kaiser ! " Napoleon was too great to claim authority of God. He put his success down to hard work, quickness of vision and action. He was profane. Greatness and profanity are allies behind the scenes. Napoleon's profanity might be called *lèse-humanité.* He denied and defied humanity. *Vox populi vox dei* was only true as it served his object—which was power. His profanity was an empirical use of religion in the systematic control of men.

Napoleon, frankest of men, was frank in this also : " How can a state be well governed without the aid of religion ? Society cannot exist save with inequality of fortune, and inequality of fortune cannot be supported without religion. When a man dies of hunger by the side of another who is gorged, he cannot accept that disparity without some authority that shall say to him : ' God has decreed it thus—there must be rich and poor in the world ; but in the hereafter, and for all eternity, it will be the other way about.' It was by becoming a Catholic that I pacified the Vendée, and a Mussulman that I established myself in Egypt ; it was by becoming ultramontane that I won over public opinion in Italy. If I ruled a people of Jews, I would rebuild the Temple of

Solomon ! Paradise is a central spot whither the souls of men proceed along different roads ; every sect has a road of its own."

But contempt of man rarely shocks us. We are only amused when a Lord Alvanley announces that he likes to sit in his club window on a Bank Holiday watching it rain on the damn people. Frederick the Great's contempt of man was shown when he rebuked a complaining and demoralized regiment with the words : " Dogs ! Would you live for ever !" What the German soldiers thought of this opinion of their will to live is not recorded. Nor in our own time has anything more than amused tolerance been aroused by Rudyard Kipling's poem in which he throws verbal vitriol at the people : " Have no truck with the beastly thing—order the guns and kill ! " Insulting mankind apparently involves no greater danger than speaking disrespectfully of the equator. At the same time, even a semi-democracy can be aroused to newspaper fury if damned openly. An instance is recorded in America, when William K. Vanderbilt uttered the famous phrase, " the Public be damned ! " over a claim for public rights in connection with the New York Central

Railway. Public conscience was shocked in England, in 1730, when one Bond, a Member of Parliament, who had been connected with a fraudulent scheme for advancing money to the poor, said, " damn the poor ! " on being informed that his victims would suffer by the failure of the scheme. In our own time a notorious " unemployed " motto : " Curse your charity—we want work ! " gave pain to numerous well-meaning philanthropists. But the honour of committing simultaneously *lèse-majesté* and *lèse-humanité* has been reserved for Bernard Shaw. He achieves the double offence very neatly in the statement, " Vulgarity in a king flatters the majority of the nation."

Profanity is not a faculty, profanity is an attitude of mind. Few men are wholly, but the best men are sometimes, profane. Profanity is revealed at its truest in the flash of an outraged soul. Like lightning, it rarely hits anything, and rarely intends to, but what it does hit is scarred or destroyed. Even when it misses it illuminates. Weak profanity, such as idle curses and cheap swearing, is, like all weak things, ineffective, futile, and beneath consideration. " Light loves

and little errors," as Swinburne said, " do not
affect the elect of heaven or hell." The present
epidemic of swearing, part of the backwash of war,
has no relation to high profanity, either in its
tragic or its comic form. It is generally no more
than the reflex action of boredom in contact with
inefficient expression. Contemporary swearing is
verbal incompetence. If every man or woman who
used that painfully overworked word " bloody "
applied it blasphemously on the basis of its alleged
derivation from " By Our Lady ! " then good folk
might well believe our generation were well on the
way to perdition—or Rome, where profanity and
Protestantism are synonymous terms.

There is a distinction, however, between sec-
tarian profanity and the august gibes and resent-
ments which periodically explode upon the page
of history. Let us not confuse this wayward child
of passion with mere heresy. The countless sects
will " furiously rage together," blaspheming one
another for blasphemy, but the profane will pass
by in the pride of humility, saving their arrows for
higher game. The sectarians are only profane to
each other as opposing neighbours are : the profane oppose themselves to the gods. They have

52

jealousy, but no littleness. Profanity is jealous of the belittlement of the gods. " I will only believe in a God who can dance," cried Nietzsche, most tragic of modern men, contemplating the sad gods of Lutheran Germany. " Beware of the man whose God is in the skies," adjures Shaw, in the face of our devastated, church-crowded civiliza-tion. " An honest god's the noblest work of man," sneers Robert Ingersoll, humorously con-temptuous of the anthropomorphic creations set up for worship by those who would trade us life-in-death for death-in-life. Beerbohm Tree's assertion that " Every man has the God he deserves " deserves to be true. Thus profanity goads the incompetent god-maker.

Profanity, being swift, flashes arrows of wit, but more from necessity than preference. Profanity is kin to humour—allied with laughter and tears. Wit is of the head; it lacks feeling, and has no pity. Humour is of the heart ; it rarely gives pain, but is always near pain, for the heart can go on feeling after it is broken. Profanity in the hour of parting laughs the soul abroad and greets death with a quip. A little before his death, Rabelais called for his domino : " Put me on my domino, for I am cold : besides, I would die in it, for *Beati qui in Domino moriuntur*," and after this most sublime of all puns he murmured, "Let down the curtain, the comedy is ended !" and so passed away. There is more bitterness but not less pathos in Heine's dying thought, " God will forgive me—that's His trade," and there is something valiant and stoical in the deathbed irritation of Thoreau. A well-meaning religious friend persisted in recalling the philosopher's thoughts to another world : " One world at a time, please !" growled Thoreau. The tragi-comedy of this rebuke is comparable with the *mot* which passed with the last breath of a reprobate nobleman who was desired by his chaplain to " call on the Lord." " I will," he replied, " if I go that way, but I don't believe I shall."

Surely there is repentance in such fatalism. But if doubt as to one's heavenly destiny has in it the elements of repentance, honest doubt of any mind cannot be entirely displeasing to any but a God made after man's image. Thus would Arthur Thistlewood, the Radical leader in the Cato Street conspiracy, have entered into bliss after such a prayer as that uttered by him on the gallows :

" O God—if there be a God—save my soul—if
I have a soul ! " Sometimes the pathos of deathbed profanity becomes holy in its very *naïveté*.
Such, for instance, as that recorded of the Spanish
patriot Ramon Narvarez, who, exhorted by the
priest to forgive his enemies, exclaimed feebly,
" My father, I have no enemies ; I have shot them
all." Nor is there less quality in profanities which
mingle impishness with tragedy. A god who could
dance, say, would welcome the delicious old French
lady, admired of George Meredith, who, when the
curé came with consolation for her last moments,
told him her best improper story, and died.

The Church has not always escaped the slings
and arrows of profanity, and often the stones have
hit and the barbs stuck, for the Church is exposed
to attack in all periods and, being human, deserves
it in most. There is something peculiarly con-
soling to those who observe with dismay the
tenancy of the House of God by the devotees of
Mammon, when they remember the brothers de
Goncourt's description of the Abbé Blompoix as
the preacher who " brought Jesus Christ within
reach of the wealthy." The well-meaning profanities of preaching are innumerable, and were we

55

robbed of them we should lose a fair proportion of our most delicious vintage humour. Two of the best of them are part of the record of that entertaining gossip, the Hon. Lionel Tollemache, who remarks that Macaulay could not have said that " no field preacher ever carried his irreverent familiarity so far as to bid the Supreme Being stop and think on the importance of the interests under His care" if the historian had heard, as Tollemache had, a *locum tenens* at Helmingham exhort his congregation to remind the Deity of the promises by which He had bound Himself. He advised them to " Entangle God in His own words ! "

Tollemache gives as a further and more direct refutation of Macaulay's opinion in the story of the opening of a Congregational Church in the West of America, where the Senior Deacon began his dedicatory address, " O Lord, it has been proved to Thee by statistics how grievously inadequate has been the religious accommodation of this city." Such patronization of God is, perhaps, pushing profanity too far, so it is a relief to turn to an amiable story more recently imported from America by Mr. E. V. Lucas, about an old trapper who was induced to attend a camp meeting. Perched on a back seat, he watched the scene, when an elderly Evangelical sister placed herself beside the old hunter, laid her hand on his arm, and asked him if he loved Jesus. He pondered for some moments and then replied thus : " Waal, ma'am, I can't go so far as to say that I love him. I can't go so far as that. But, by gosh, I'll say this— I ain't got nothin' agin him." This has the correct *bouquet.*

The teaching of religion has as many humours as it has stupidities and cruelties. And while we laugh or smile, for the humour is quiet and reflective rather than rollicking, we seem to feel our way to the heart of that restlessness which makes saviours or saved of us all. The story of the slightly deaf old lady who, according to Bernard Shaw, sat for years at the feet of Charles Bradlaugh at the Hall of Science, under the impression that the famous Atheist was a Methodist, shows that, as Omar believed, only a hair divides the false and true. And one lingers over the memory of Talleyrand's advice to Lepaux, the inventor of a new religion called Theophilanthropy, with justifiable malice. Lepaux complained that France was not exactly eager to adopt the new gospel. Talleyrand replied sympathetically, " I am not surprised at the difficulty you experience ; it is no easy matter to introduce a new religion ; but I will tell you what you might, at any rate, try : I recommend you to be crucified and to rise again on the third day." Profanity, not for the first time, jumps down on the side of religion. Indeed, profanity loses point and piquancy when completely separated from reverence. Profanity is not irreverence, it is outraged reverence. The world may yet be saved by a profane saint.[1]

[1] Since writing these words my attention has been drawn to a valuable elucidation of this passage in the essay on Baudelaire in the third volume of *La Vie Littéraire*, which I cannot deny myself the pleasure of quoting. M. France says :

" I am not wrong, therefore, in saying that he [Baudelaire] is a Christian. But one must add that Baudelaire, like M. Barbey d'Aurévilly, is a very bad Christian. He loves sin, and delightedly enjoys the voluptuousness of falling. He knows that he is damning himself, and in that he pays a homage to divine wisdom, which will be accounted to him for righteousness, but he has the vertigo of damnation, and no taste for women, beyond that sufficient surely to lose his soul. He is never a lover, and he would not even be a debauchee if debauchery were not superlatively impious. He is much less attached to the form than to the spirit, which he regards as diabolical. He would leave women completely alone, were it not that he hopes thereby to offend God and make the angels weep.

" Such ideas are doubtless perverse enough, and I see that they

We can only guess what is in the mind of God, just as we can only guess the purpose of life. But without committing the cheap sin of making God in our own image, we may venture the opinion that, if God has preferences in these glimpses of the moon, those preferences would be for human character which displayed spirit as well as spirituality. The timid acceptors of fate might

distinguished Baudelaire from those old monks who sincerely dreaded the phantoms of the night. Pride was what had thus depraved Baudelaire. In his arrogance he wished that everything he did, even his most trivial impurities, should be important ; he was glad that they were sins, because they would attract the attention of heaven and hell. Fundamentally, he was never more than half a believer. His temperament alone was wholly Christian. His heart and intellect remained empty. It is said that one day a friend, a naval officer, showed him a *ju-ju* which he had brought back from Africa, a monstrous little head carved in wood by a negro.

" ' Well, it's very ugly,' said the sailor, and he threw it contemptuously aside.

" ' Take care,' said Baudelaire uneasily. ' Suppose it were really a god ! '

" They were the most profane words he had ever spoken. He believed in the unknown gods, especially for the pleasure of blaspheming. To sum up, I do not think that Baudelaire ever had a perfectly clear idea of the state of soul which I have tried to define. But it seems to me that one finds, amid incredible puerilities and ridiculous affectations, a truly sincere testimony in his work."—*On Life and Letters*, by Anatole France. Translated by D. B. Stewart, pp. 22-23.

59

conceivably give place to those valiant ones who, rather than barter their soul for eternal bliss, defied even the Most High if they felt aggrieved, and died with a laugh or, if needs be, a taunt on their lips. An honest God would welcome honest profanities even in those who could not honestly believe in him, especially, one would like to think, if the rogue of an infidel had the spirit of a Stendhal, who, visualizing the sin and pain of this world, said, "The only excuse for God is that he does not exist ! " And even such an honest God might conceivably laugh with us at some profanity revealed in a flash of humour. This is more doubtful, for your gods are grim folk, despite Heine's assertion that God was " the Aristophanes of Heaven." But the Elysian Fields must be duller than the least enthusiastic devotee imagines if the gods were not to be moved at least to benign smiles by the record of the assembly of philosophers which was held in Heaven when one of them went up to God and whispered confidentially, " Between friends, we do not believe that you exist at all," a profanity equalled only by the enthusiasm of the Hyde Park orator who thanked God he was an Atheist !

But mere doubt is a poor form of profanity. It is so obvious and so easy as to be almost innocuous. High profanity springs from tragic wrath or exalted pity, and is revealed oftener in art than life. Dionysos is the god of profanity : " beautiful but ineffectual angel beating in the void his luminous wings in vain."

There is dignity in objection involving disfavour or disgrace, whether of God or man. There is dignity also in unshrinking acquiescence when untoward fate or circumstance conquers. But few can maintain their dignity under stress of beatitude. Tragedy dignifies. Destiny, though still mysterious even to the modern mind, is mysterious only as a familiar disease is mysterious ; and, like a disease, it is attacked and exploded, cajoled and circumvented. Oracles foretell its evolution and priests devise illusions to give the doomed courage. But none have yet answered the profane and bitter realism of ancient Greece. " I was not, I came to be : I was, I am not : that is all ; and who shall say more, will lie : I shall not be," sang an unknown poet ; and Palladas mourned, " We are all watched and fed for Death as a herd of swine butchered wantonly " ; and Glycon's, " All is laughter, and all is dust, and all is nothing ; for out of unreason is all that is." [1] Thus, the tragic attitude of the finite towards the infinite down the ages.

The essence of tragedy is purification by contest with unknown forces. Tragedy places a nimbus about the brows of the doomed. Whether it be Greek or Renaissance, Hebrew or modern European, tragedy is always a revelation of the sanctity of the pain-forged, the transcendentalism of sorrow. Thus, we are permitted to contemplate the great tragic figures of Œdipus and Dionysos, Jesus and Job, Tintagiles and Deirdre and Peer Gynt. And in the less real life which we live it is always those who have battled against great odds and failed who are sublime. Success alone is commonplace.

Profanity becomes sublime when it is thus allied, when, like Shadrach, Meshach, and Abednego, it walks unscathed through the fiery furnace of tragedy. When profanity is plaintive it is weak, but it is saved from contemptible weakness by courage. The craven and the fearful can be neither

[1] These three translations are from Mackail's *Select Epigrams from the Greek Anthology*.

tragic nor profane. Better set God a good example
than beg for mercy :

> *Here lie I, Martin Elginbrod:*
> *Have mercy on my soul, Lord God,*
> *As I wad do were I Lord God*
> *And ye were Martin Elginbrod.*

Many have felt so, and the old Scottish epitaph is
not unique, for the same thought finds expression
elsewhere, notably in Edward FitzGerald's quat-
rain after Omar Khayyam :

> *Oh, Thou, who Man of baser Earth didst make,*
> *And who with Eden didst devise the Snake;*
> *For all the Sin wherewith the Face of Man*
> *Is blacken'd, Man's forgiveness give—and take!*

It is not without significance that most notable
examples of exalted profanity are drawn from other
days than ours. May we assume that, as ribaldry
takes the place of outraged reverence, and
cynicism that of faith, profanity will become a
lost art ?

The profanities of the war have yet to be
recorded : the harvest should be profuse. Meanwhile, that stupendous event is too near for

detailed realization. The impression is massive and confused, a tangled panorama of events with noisy accompaniments rather than the revelation of soul and character in immortal phrases. Little khaki-clad troops with pink faces swinging along high roads and streets to the sound of hymn tunes set to words so obscene that they will never be printed . . . curses and laughter, always laughter and always curses . . . and, arising out of the confusion and noise, appeals to God, patronization of God, the conscription of God by all combatants:

God heard the embattled nations sing and shout
"Gott strafe England!" and "God save the King!"
God this, God that, and God the other thing—
"Good God!" said God, "I've got my work cut out!"

The profane bitterness of Mr. Squire's epigram springs from the same source as the ribaldry of our soldiers—and all nations' soldiers—in that great tragedy. The embattled nations mobilized their Gods, men and goods.

When Montaigne, the honest father of the essay, found his opinions opposed to those of the Church, and himself in danger of pontifical displeasure, he circumvented trouble by informing His Holiness that the essays contained only his private opinions and not his opinions as a Catholic. Profanity is private opinion kicking over the traces. It may happen to the worst of us, and the best. Montaigne was a good man in the best sense of the word, as Mr. Gladstone was once described as a good man in the worst sense of the word. Montaigne was orthodox and yet profane. Arthur Hugh Clough was as good and as, or even more, conventional, yet he was profane enough to re-write the Ten Commandments in terms appropriate to the nineteenth century of the true faith. Clough's Decalogue is probably more popular, even though it is denied a thousand times a day, than that which Moses brought down from Sinai. The Sermon on the Mount we know would not withstand the acid test so well, for :

John P. Robinson, he
Said they didn't know everything
Down in Judee.

No one would seem to be the worse for profanity, or the better except, perchance, the profane, some of whom may, at least, have enjoyed themselves. We can imagine the indignant pleasure a certain Lord Durham got out of the record of a fire made in his diary to the effect that Almighty God is supposed to have caused the conflagration—"for reasons best known to Himself." To complain without a cause is pleasant, but how much more than pleasant must be the feeling you experience when you hurl your barbed words at the fate which has destroyed your hope or checkmated your desire! We all have observed with what unfeigned delight some ladies indulge in the gentle art of what is called giving her, or him, a piece of their mind. Let us leave the profane this little solace, for it is all they will get. Yes, profanity is its own reward. And in the last reckoning, if there be a last reckoning, we may discover that God has paid even less attention to His critics and satirists than men have paid to the sneers of their Alvanleys and Fredericks. The pathos of profanity is its helplessness.

THE TRIUMPH OF FEAR

I STOOD once upon a pier-head and watched some small fishing boats being tossed and shaken by the unseen hands of a storm. Behind me lay the harbour, calmly nestling between the strong, sheltering arms of the granite breakwater. In there the ships were at peace, swaying lazily at their moorings or moving easily and safely about their business with quiet indifference to the threats of the gale. And as I turned again towards the fury of the open sea I thought of the genius which went to the creation of the masonry behind me : the genius by which the sea had been conquered and tamed.

The harbour, like all harbours, had about it the inevitability and simplicity of supreme human achievement, and I thought that the beings who could imagine and contrive such a piece of work could imagine and contrive anything. Pondering thus, my fancy ranged over the wide field of human ingenuity : wonder after wonder passed before me, but not the wonders usually sung by

67

poets. I saw elements and forces of nature—fire
and steam and electricity, curbed by the will of
man ; fierce gases touched to light ; objects and
sounds recorded on sensitive plates for the delight and instruction of the eye and the ear ;
human messages thrown magically round the
world ; wonders of locomotion, aviation, biology,
chemistry, surgery—and yet, withal this endless
procession of miracles, I was filled only with
desolation.

Man, lord of so great a realm, master of so
many things, controller of storms, director of
whirlwinds, exploiter of savage lightning and con-
suming fire ; lord of a hundred energies and
magician of untold mysteries, had yet contrived
no secure harbour for his body, no inevitable
temple for his soul. Man, the lord of creation, the
paragon of animals, infinite in faculty, angelic in
action, godlike in apprehension—tossed hither and
thither, unsettled in the midst of his wonders ;
man, self-appointed wonder of the world, was yet
the creature of his own fears, the destroyer of his
own peace.

When he had to save a ship or tunnel a mountain or girdle the earth with communicating nerves

he became a Titan ; when he created a symphony
or an epic, a Parthenon or a York Minster, he
became a god ; but when he had to save himself
he reverted to the ape—to less than the ape.
Humanity seems capable of everything save the
building of a fair and reasonably secure haven for
itself.

But we are too human to judge these tragic
reactions, too much involved in them to condemn,
and, on the whole, enjoying the capricious game
too well to do more than indulge a passing complaint. We live more or less happily in a fantastic
tragedy illuminated by flashes of comedy, and
salted, for palates that have not grown too coarse
in the struggle, with irony. Civilization is a
fortuitous game of beggar-my-neighbour—a paradoxical accumulating of power immediately to be
scattered and wasted. We seem to build but to
destroy, to arrange but to disarrange, to create not
order out of chaos but chaos out of order. We
applaud progress without progressing and without
having any clear idea towards that which we would
progress ; we worship the Prince of Peace and are
continually at war ; we fight for freedom and
achieve a new slavery ; we demand increased

production of goods and coincidentally increase prices to such an extent that we are unable to consume what we produce. . . These are but specimens, incidents in the queer game.

Yet, in spite of the paradoxical scattering of forces, we lack neither the sense of unity nor the spirit of goodwill. Civilization is out to unify and unite everybody and everything—but itself; we are overwhelmed by well-meaning : Hell, it has been observed, is paved with good intentions—not bad.

Our age is extraordinarily rich in vision ; it does not lack soul. The trouble is that it cannot practise what it dreams, and has long since given up even pretending to practise what it preaches. Language was never more a means of disguising thought than it is now ; it requires an expert to distinguish newspaper news from propaganda, and the wildest political outburst is often no more than a masquerade. Considering these things there are those who declaim against our intelligence ; but it is as absurd to say that we lack ideas as to say that we lack skill. The world was never more richly endowed with brains and ability : we can imagine anything—and do ; and do anything

70

—and don't. I saw in an American journal the other day one of those crisp pieces of pocket-wisdom which are America's most original contribution to modern thought, to the effect that those who made a habit of picture theatres had nowhere else to go but home. How typical of the modern world—man has nowhere to go but home, and home is insufferable ! The situation recalls a famous Phil May drawing of a drunken man who, upon being recalled from the house of refreshment to the domestic hearth by a forbidding but justly indignant wife, replied that he would do anything in reason—but he would not go home. Civilization will do anything in reason, but it will not put its house in order : perhaps it cannot.

Modern life is an attenuated night out : we cannot even arrive home with the milk, like gentlemen. Is it possible that we are frightened ? There have been many attempts to explain the cause or causes of the Great War, but no one, so far as I have read or heard, has gone further or deeper than to put the blame on someone else. This is natural, and comforting. There is nothing so agreeable in life as to unload your faults upon the just and unjust alike. The fact that you are, in Mr.

Dooley's words, " a liar, and know you are," does not destroy the pleasure. Stripped of such illusions we should feel as though we had been stripped of our clothes. Illusions may be the figleaves of civilization : but they are illusions none the less. What then if we awoke one of these fine mornings and discovered that the cause of the Great War was not someone else but our fear of each other ? The cause of the Great War was Cowardice! It is worth consideration, for the war did not begin in 1914 and end in 1918—it began with man, and will end only when man becomes something better than a Yahoo.

Fear as a mainspring of human endeavour is an inheritance from our cousins of the animal world. At one time it was the corner-stone of religion. Men were taught to fear God, and they crucified for a dangerous fanatic the inspired being who made the revolutionary pronouncement : God is love. The God of the Hebrews could not have been more jealous than man, and, to do him credit, he never succeeded in inspiring so much fear for himself as men have inspired in each other. Fear is the dominant characteristic of our time. Little is achieved without it. Fear of disease makes us ill. The bricks of Harley Street are cemented with fear. Fear of revolution scares our furtive reactionaries into futile reformers. Soviet Russia is the child of fear, conceived in fear, and fed on fear. Fear of autocracy and fear of democracy, fear of war and fear of peace ; fear of Germany and France and Poland and Ukrainia and Finland and England and Japan and—Russia ; fear of rich men and poor men, peasant and plutocrat, Lenin and Trotsky. Russia is the triumph of fear. But the possibilities of fear are equally distributed throughout civilization. America's fear of the yellow race and the black race is pregnant with as much chaos as Ulster's fear of Sinn Fein or Sinn Fein's fear of Ulster. But we need not go abroad for examples ; fearfulness begins at home. We have examples in our own Parliament where every decision is determined by one or the other of these three fears : Fear of the voter (to whom the politician has usually lied, out of fear of being defeated at the polls) ; fear of private interests (to which the Party Funds are indebted); and fear of revolution (which would destroy everything by a new gamut of fears).

Could we only destroy our fears we should be

better equipped for the fight. " It is fear I stand most in fear of," said Montaigne, most wise and most frank of essayists. The attitude has the excellence of virtue, even though it lacks the splendour of courage. To fear only fear is much ado about nothing, like being in love with beauty or truth rather than being beautiful or true ; worshipping goodness and being good for nothing. There is no health in the worship or fear of such abstractions. Fear in itself is nothing ; but fear of each other is cowardice. Those who fight because they are frightened fight blindly. Most of us are fighting blindly and making a pretty mess of the world.

Life is a battle, with intervals for repose and refreshment. But the battle of life so far as man is concerned should be waged against the enemies of mankind—death, ignorance, and disease—and not against man. Civilization as we practise it is the art of putting the punch in the wrong place.

THE ADVANTAGE OF BEING
PREJUDICED

I N the newspapers, and in all common argument and opinion, there is perhaps no mental
state so belittled and despised as that known as
prejudice. To say " he is prejudiced " is enough
to condemn any man. I have known people with
a prejudice against prejudice grow violent even in
their denunciation of prejudiced persons. By far
the majority of these objectors, however, pronounce
their ban in a curt word or so, dismissing it quietly
with a superior gesture befitting a conclusion
which has invincible logic on its side. For myself
I am imperturbable in the face of rational things.
I incline to look with suspicion upon all objections
to the failings of others because I perceive a
subtle pleasure in the blaming of others for those
weaknesses which we secretly cherish in ourselves.
For instance, what we call meanness in others we
call carefulness, economy, thrift, and other high-
sounding names in ourselves. Stubbornness in
another is firmness in us ; to be logically against

us is to be unreasonable. It has occurred to me, therefore, that the same fate may have happened to this maligned thing, prejudice.

It is a curious fact that people are always surprised at the existence of prejudice ; they seem amazed that anyone should be so foolish as to be prejudiced. Nevertheless, the habit is so universal that if it had been fundamentally evil society and all its institutions ought to have been wrecked without the help of the Great War. For are not all men prejudiced about something ?

Some of the world's greatest men have been prejudiced about most things ; and all women specialize in prejudice—that is one reason why they are so delightful and so exasperating. But let us consider for a moment the mechanism of this disreputable thing. We say that a man is prejudiced when he is not open to reason. And so he is. But is that wrong ? When you jump into a river to save a drowning child, you do not reason about your action. If you did you would leave the child to its fate. There is every reason why you should. You have a wife ; you have children of your own ; you have a business dependent upon you ; you are subject to rheumatism and to chills, and you cannot swim. These are all excellent reasons for keeping on dry land and endeavouring to fish the brat out with a boat-hook. But you throw reason to the winds, and jump into the water because you are prejudiced in favour of saving life at any cost, even at the cost of your own life and the happiness of those who have showered their love upon you.

But it is not my desire to prove that prejudice is always right, nor yet to beg the question by saying that it is not always wrong. Prejudice, like everything else, can be both right and wrong, and it can be both at the same time according to the prejudice of the onlooker. But prejudice has more chance of being right than any mere display of reason. My reason for this belief (and I am prepared to admit it is unreasonable to be so reasonable) is that prejudice springs from those instincts which are at the source of life. It has the spontaneity of life. Look at the animals. Do they reason about things ? Not a bit of it. They just act from prejudice and chance their luck ; and this habit does not seem to have interfered with their evolution. Look at man ! When the first animal took it into its head to be reasonable it

77

became a human being, and its descendants seem to have devoted the rest of their time to quarrelling over the prejudices of each other, whilst clinging valiantly to their own. This is the point where Nature asserts herself in the complex artificiality of civilization. She sees that the spontaneous, the instinctive, the irrational things survive, and in our own moments of wisdom we agree with her by calling our prejudice intuition and faith. If you go among rationalists—that is, people who have a conscientious and reasonable objection to all prejudices but their own—you will find that they pronounce faith as among the unpardonable sins. They have every right to do so, but they are quite wrong in believing that their reasonableness settles the question. It does nothing of the sort; and reason ought to have taught them that the bad name that hangs a dog one day may save a dog the next. So it is with prejudice.

In a convincing proportion of cases our attacks upon prejudice are simple attacks upon reason. For no matter how reasonable a man may be in defence of his whims or beliefs or preferences, if he is proof against your own reason you conclude that he is prejudiced. You overlook the important

78

fact that you have been arguing with him in the hope of converting him to your own point of view. But it does not matter, because when you call him prejudiced he returns the compliment. We all resent conclusions which can be proved up to the hilt, but which we still know to be wrong. That is the thing we usually denounce under the name of prejudice. But that thing is not prejudice at all. It is logic. Most of the abominable things in the world have been done in its name. Nothing was more rational than the Spanish Inquisition —except, perhaps, Prussian militarism. The upholders of these systems could prove their reasonableness up to the last turn of the thumbscrew and the last strut of the Goose Stepper, but all their logic cannot intimidate the universal prejudice that their acts were cruel, brutal, and brutalizing. Cruelty may be logically necessary, but it can never be humanly right.

Nothing was so remarkable in the eruption of vituperation born of the war, and nothing did so much to make the tragic catastrophe popular among all combatants, than the charges brought by one nation against another. We, and the French, denounced the Germans as barbarians,

and they returned the compliment by yelling
" mercenary " at us and " degenerate " at our co-
partners in the contest across the Straits of Dover.
We were all very logical and very wrong. There is
much that is barbarous in your German, but his
barbaric gifts did not make the war. There are
many degenerates in France, almost as many as
there are in England, but the French are over-
whelmingly sane and healthy as a nation, and
infinitely more far-seeing and calculating than the
Germans. And as for ourselves, the charge of
mercenariness misses our national characteristic
with customary German obtuseness, not because we
are not mercenary—we share that quality with the
civilization which exalts money as the symbol of
value and the test of joy—but because in the last
resort we are, as a nation, moved by sentiment and
prejudice more than by any other thing. The only
difference between ourselves and the Germans is
that we felt about the war and were right, and that
they reasoned about the war and were wrong. We
had an inborn and instinctive prejudice against
militarism—Germany had a cultured and logically evolved conviction that militarism would make
them the inheritors and rulers of Europe. For-

tunately for Europe and the world, Britain's stalwart prejudices stood as bulwarks against that sort of thing.

Shakespeare may have had many reasons for writing *Hamlet*, but one of them must have been a desire to prove that if the Prince of Denmark had not been so reasonable all would have been well, and we should have been spared the carnival of death in the last act. It was Hamlet's capacity for thinking himself out of his instinctive preferences that made the great tragedy possible. And this same cause is behind half the tragedies of our daily lives. It is behind the tragedy of dullness. Just imagine a world that was not afraid of being unreasonable. What variety we should have, what unimaginable interest in life, what undreamt-of battles!

For it is not peace we want in this world, but variety of contest. We want the sword, but not always the sword of steel, excellent as that is. We want swords of wit and wisdom and imagination. And we want the sword of faith—no matter in what cause. Good faith justifies any cause. And to get these we must never be ashamed of our prejudices. Indeed, when all is said and done, and this argument sent to limbo, the predestined home of all arguments, prejudice will be found laughing over the ruins of intellect—for, if prejudice is not life, prejudice is nine points of the law of life.

WHY DO WE LAUGH?

VIRTUES are as mysterious as they are admirable, and not least among them, both for strangeness and excellence, is laughter. What is this laughter which has " puzzled the philosophers so much to explain " ? Why do we laugh ?—" *No voice will tell,*" answers the poet :

No voice will tell:
No God, no Demon of severe response,
Deigns to reply from Heaven or from Hell.

Many have tried to answer the question, but the best answers are drowned in laughter as we fall back on the popular, but none the less wise, assumption that, inexplicable as it may be, laughter is somehow good.

We are reputedly a laughing people. The reputation is not unearned. We laugh and cry, or, rather, growl, alternately—laugh till we cry, and cry till we laugh—cry about nothing, and laugh about everything. Laugh at ourselves, for ourselves, and by ourselves. England is a democracy of laughter. If God, as Heine asserted, was the Aristophanes of Heaven, and Heine himself, as he asserted again, the Aristophanes of Germany, then surely John Bull is the Aristophanes of Europe.

For an Englishman does not laugh merely at what he has made or unmade, or at those with whom he has to live: he laughs at those he has to kill, and, more hilarious still, at those who wish to kill him. If he does not laugh at his Creator, he certainly laughs with him. Nietzsche said he would only believe in a dancing God ; John Bull, a saner philosopher, believes in a laughing God. So far as my researches go there is only one form of Christian ritual in which you are permitted to laugh ; it is to be found in those very joyous gatherings of the Salvation Army invented by that stalwart Englishman William Booth, who, "from his abode where the eternal are," may surely claim to have been the first to have brought laughter into the service of the Lord :

> *The banjos rattled and the tambourines*
> *Jing-jing-jingled in the hands of Queens.*

We not only laugh but we like laughing, and we peacock ourselves on the ease and readiness of our good-humoured explosions. You can test this statement. Tell any one of us that we lack a sense of humour—and watch the result. Conversely, watch us swell with satisfaction as often as we are told that the Scots are lacking in that sense. We are never tired of recalling Sydney Smith's defamation of Scottish character—which probably shows that we are not nearly so gifted in humour as we think we are. Tell an Englishman that he is not a gentleman and he will think you are jealous ; tell him he is illogical and he will think you a fool ; but say he has no sense of humour and he will think you are mad.

The cause of this pride is as difficult to explain as the cause of laughter itself. Keats was an English poet, but he could not solve the problem of his own laughter. Nor can I solve the problem of our English laughter. It is there, it is generally good-hearted, and that is all we know about it. But if we cannot answer why we laugh, we can note some of the queer things we laugh at and laugh while we marvel at the laughter they arouse. Of course, I am aware that as a race we are by no means monopolists of laughter. Laughter is one of the characteristics common to all men and, if

we except the putative partnership of the hyena
and the jackass, not shared with the animal world.
But the laughing hyena and the laughing jackass
are not full partners, they are only co-partners, for
the noises they make bear but a superficial resemblance to the laughter of mankind. The curious
effect of this fortuitous resemblance, rather than
the resemblance itself, marks the unbridgeable
gulf of laughter which separates man and beast.
When we hear of a horse or a pig or a dog showing
signs of reason we are agreeably surprised, we look
upon it as a compliment—nature catching up ;
but when the hyena laughs we are disturbed, as
we are when a bad man laughs. It is in our favour
that we like to feel good when we laugh. " Laugh
and grow fat" is one of our old sayings, and, sure
enough, one of the penalties of goodness, if only
goodness to yourself, is *embonpoint!* We respect
the lean ascetic, and sometimes forgive him, but
humanity ranges itself on the side of the plump
and jovial as though they symbolized that
Kingdom of God which is within each one of us.

You may know a man by his laugh more surely
than by his words or his gestures, the clothes he
wears or the friends he keeps. When we laugh

spontaneously we drop the mask as completely as if we were in our cups. But laughter can be a mask as well. How well Dickens had observed this is revealed in the sinister grinning of his Carkers and Uriah Heeps. But this is an unpleasant subject, so we shall leave such creatures to grin themselves away like the Cheshire Cat in *Alice in Wonderland.* And for the same reason let us pass those others who laugh ironically or sardonically, pausing but to record our recognition of the Mephistophelian right to its own technique.

Nor is the manner of our laughter very pertinent to our theme ; we seek rather the cause thereof. At the same time the curious and diligent always find satisfaction in working backwards from effects to causes whether those causes be first or last, lost or merely elusive. Thus may a flower-like tenderness have inspired the mighty quakes which on slender prompting shook the sides, and the environment, of Walter Savage Landor. He laughed long and loud and lived to a great age, which suggests a fruitful and helpful digression into laughter as a healer. Laugh and grow fat, so long as you do not pass beyond reasonable and agreeable plumpness, may be another way of saying laugh and live long. Should man, as some affirm, and not without good argument, be no more (and no less, for it is a miracle all the same) than the result of a chemical formula which one of these days we shall analyse with scientific precision, then it would be easy to determine the effect of laughter on his constituent elements. We seek laughter in moments of gloom. What does it do to us when it " cheers us up " ? Is laughter anti-toxical ? Does it intimidate the *phagocytes* ? Can one laugh an army of *streptococci* out of one's internal realms, or beat the *coli* beyond one's frontiers by a big push of merriment ? If so, doctors of medicine must look to their laurels, or ultimately give place to doctors of humour. How charming it would be to go to a Harley Street re-populated with humourists, to read on those sleek and ominous brass plates names like Mark Twain and Stephen Leacock instead of Sir Arbuthnot Lane or Sir Frederick Treves ! To go there half healed by anticipation because you know that your dolour and not your *colon* is to be short-circuited, your gloom and not your *vermiform appendix* nipped in the bud ; and even though you go without hope of reprieve, for we all must die sooner or later, your heart is light in the opportunity of being tickled to death by some master stroke of humour. Come, then, genial anæsthetists of the soul, wreathe Harley Street in smiles, awaken Wimpole Street with your mirth, heal us with humour, make us whole with hilarity, so that we may live long and kindly, and, dying, laugh at Death !

Some of the greatest servants of humanity have rarely laughed, and some of the worst have been notorious laughers. Wordsworth was not a laughing man ; nor was Swift. Alexander Pope was devoid of all merriment. Keats, on the other hand, was gay of heart before he was stricken with disease, and in our own time George Meredith laughed as greatly as he wrote. Lord Chesterfield disapproved of laughter. It was low and unbecoming. He bragged that nobody had ever heard him laugh. But this need not perturb us. I for one am content not to have heard his lordship laugh, for if I had I know I should have been deprived of this apostle of gentility's delicious *Letters* to his son. Dr. Johnson, however, laughed much, approved of laughter in others, and was not afraid of measuring a man by his mirth. Yet from such diversities it were unwise to make any deductions towards our argument.

Nor may we hope to find help from the manner of men's laughter. Dr. Johnson is said to have laughed like a rhinoceros. Boswell called it " a good-humoured growl." Swinburne screeched like a parakeet. One of the merriest souls of my acquaintance shut his eyes when amused and made a noise like a death rattle. Some have sibilant laughter, others cluck ; some croak like the raven, others gurgle ; there are gobbling laughers, and laughers who simmer and simper, which are two distinct operations ; some neigh like horses, or grunt like pigs, or snuffle like asthmatics. You may laugh like crying. Laughter also may have inwardness: it may be sinister, naughty, bibulous, satirical, bilious, hectic, simian, hysterical, abandoned, profane, exalted, Rabelaisian, Homeric, or Shavian.

Much laughter is nameless and unaccountable: laughter in Courts of Justice and at public meetings. In the House of Commons laughter is often ripe inanity : the outward and visible sign of an inward and spiritual—space. Perhaps it is nerves —perhaps, just nothing reacting from nothing

. . . malnutrition of ideas . . . wind-blown boredom . . . Mass laughter is different. An audience moved by a George Robey or a Charles Chaplin is like a wood out of which all the dead boughs are being shaken by a cleansing gale. (George Robey—cleansing! did I hear you exclaim? Yes, my dear young lady of the male persuasion, cleansing. Have you never laughed at Robey as he walked across the stage—are not his silences even the funniest happenings in these islands? But what about the things he says? Vulgar? Of course—and so were Rabelais and Shakespeare and Sterne—when they had a mind to it, which was when they thought their public wanted it—you see, mass humour . . . but that belongs to the body of the essay, not to this parenthesis.) There is something strengthening in mass laughter. It is easily aroused and quickly stilled, but while it lasts it unites like a sacrament, and, unlike more " religious " communalizations of the feelings, there are no unpleasant reactions. Indeed, laughter is a social and socializing act, it is the only form of solidarity which has justified itself in practice. Nothing is so annoying as to hear others laughing without knowing why or being able to join them; and only the imbecile makes a habit of laughing by himself. Laughter must be shared to be enjoyed.

Yet the things that make us laugh are neither always good nor always kind. Humour is often cruel, though the laughter it arouses is generally kind. The most popular ingredients of humour are the real or imaginary troubles of our fellow men—and women. A fat man in difficulties is an unfailing mirth-maker at all times.

It is, perhaps, not without significance that our greatest literary creator expended the fullness of his sense of humour upon the conception of Sir John Falstaff, who, amiable rogue and braggart though he was, and despicable as he would be in the minds of most who laugh at him in the theatre were they to meet him in real life, is actually a tragi-comic figure, the figure of a goodly, portly man, and a corpulent in trouble. So successful was Sir John Falstaff in the theatre of the Shake-spearean era that the box-office demanded a repetition of the success, and Shakespeare complied by making his fat knight appear in no fewer than four plays, in one of which his troubles are the sole theme.[1] But it is not only in Shakespeare that this association of humour and trouble is to be found. To come nearer our own day, we shall find the same characteristics related in those great humorous conceptions of Charles Dickens, Mr. Pickwick and Mr. Micawber. These two amiable gentlemen were always in trouble, and if you stripped their troubles away from them there would be nothing left for laughter and little for any other purpose. The comic spirit of Meredith was engaged with the same theme, and the more humorous he became, as in such characters as the Great Mel and Richmond-Roy, the more his characters became dependent upon troubles, even if those troubles were only the characteristic English troubles of the snob.

The same tendency may be noted in still more modern English humour. It is the essence of most of the humorous conceptions of Mr. H. G. Wells, who possesses, among other admirable qualities, the quality of being one of the most pro-

[1] Shakespeare knew what he was doing, for he makes Falstaff say : " The brain of this foolish-compounded clay, man, is not able to invent anything that tends to laughter more than I invent or is invented on me : I am not only witty in myself, but the cause that wit is in other men."—2 *Henry IV*, Act I, Sc. 2.

93

found of living humourists. What are Kipps and Mr. Polly, and even the monumental Mr. Ponderevo, but distracted mortals courting further distraction in the illusion of money-power ? And again, if you turn to our black-and-white art you will find that in the best of it—in the best work of Phil May, for instance—you are laughing at the troubles and even the tragedies of life. Phil May never rose to such heights of irresistible humour as when he was depicting subjects that ought to have reduced us to tears. Why do we laugh at his " sketch from life " representing a most disastrous family of street singers wailing " We're a rare old—fair old—rickety, rackety crew " ? Phil May made England rock with merriment over his Dottyville series of jokes about lunatics. . . .

A contemporary of the great black-and-white artist, Dan Leno, expressed much the same point of view on the stage. English music-halls vibrated with delight as that inimitable artist represented the trials and tribulations of simple folk. James Welch, who came nearer the spirit of true comedy, obeyed the same unwritten law. I always felt that the laughter provoked by his characterization in *The Man in the Street* was an expression of relief from the underlying tragedy of the thing. But if there is any doubt about that, there could be no doubt whatever about the small gasps of hysterical laughter during his realistic interpretation of the condemned man in Gilbert's little tragedy *The Hooligan*. The theme is so painful as to be almost unbearable. I have seen people walk out in the midst of this play unable to stand any more of it. Yet those who remained in the grip of the horror, watching Welch revealing the fear of a condemned man during his supposed last few moments on earth—the fear of a man who is half idiot, and who has very little worth preserving in his life—those who remained laughed every now and then at the humour of it. Some things may be too deep for tears, but nothing is too deep for laughter. Charles Lamb, gentlest of souls, said " anything awful " made him laugh.

Paradoxical as it may seem, humour is apparently a solemn business. Laughter may be—indeed, in certain phases it is—little more than the expression of a sort of emotional cannibalism. The idea is uproariously supported by Gilbert's picture of the entrancing cannibal who was the only survivor of the good ship *Nancy Bell* :

Oh, I am a cook and a captain bold,
  And the mate of the " Nancy " brig,
And a bo'sun tight, and a midshipmite,
  And the crew of the captain's gig.

Just as this fine fellow survived from the wreck by eating the crew of his boat, so perhaps we survive the tragedy of life by laughing.

Many have tried to answer Keats's question without making much progress, and as many more have tried to solve the riddle of laughter. The consensus of opinion, though differing in every imaginable detail, after the manner of philosophic conclusions, agrees in the main upon one point—a point, it is worth nothing, that has long since been settled by popular belief. Laughter is generally believed to be a good thing. It is as good for men to have a good laugh as it is for women to have a good cry. Perhaps the two functions are related. Bergson's researches into the causes and uses of laughter support the idea. Laughter for him is a corrective—but so are tears. Laughter, he says, would fail in its object if it bore the stamp of sympathy or kindness ; its business is to intimidate by humiliating. " By laughter society avenges itself for the liberties taken with it." All of which is interesting, and may be true, but it leaves us bewildered when we recall our tears ; for what are they doing, big and little ones, and not solely those Tennysonian tears " from the depths of some divine despair," if not avenging some liberty that society or fate or circumstance has taken with us ? The acute but genial " Autocrat of the Breakfast Table " here comes to our aid. " Laughter and tears," he says, " are meant to turn the wheels of the same sensibility : one is wind-power and the other water-power, that is all." But that does not explain laughter, it only gives it relation. Is laughter inexplicable, like so many good things ? Not to try to understand laughter, but to laugh, is doubtless the soundest advice. By so doing we may yet save ourselves the ignominy of being laughed out of the court of life.

Lest it be thought that I am an advocate of indiscriminate laughter, I had better, perhaps, end with a warning. Laughter is sometimes unnecessary, sometimes out of place, sometimes preposterous, and, as often as not, the mark of the human jackass. " It may seem strange," says wise Thomas Fuller, "that, *risible* being the property of man alone, they who have least of man should have most thereof." When I praise laughter, therefore, I mean the laughter of the brimming heart, the laughter of the buoyant spirit and the bright keen brain—not the insensate giggle or the ribald guffaw. Although in the mass we laugh at everything, individuals discriminate ; not always consciously, but instinctively. And, according to the quality of personality and the range and distinction of experience, laughter will be rich and eloquent. That sort of laughter will also be rare. Great laughter is allied with reverence. Healthy laughter is more in the nature of self-criticism. Bad laughter is either the expression of mere emptiness of mind and soul or the sign of malice and resentment. " The stroke of the great humourist," says Meredith, " is world-wide, with lights of Tragedy in his laughter." Laughter, it would appear, is no laughing matter ; it springs from the still-deeps of seriousness. Only the dolt is content to laugh and grow fat ; those who are anything or stand for anything prefer to laugh and grow wise. Observing this, we may agree with Chamfort when he says that " the most wasted of all days is that on which one has not laughed."

STANDING BY POSTERITY

MORALLY, I am on the side of posterity, but I would not push this partiality too far; there is reasonableness, which is better than mere reason, in all things, and we must have a care lest our desire to safeguard the interests of those who come after us conflict with our object and, at the same time, lead us into useless sacrifices of present opportunities of that fuller life which is even now overdue: We must refrain from making a god of our posterity. This argument, unspoken often, is felt by all.

It has no faults as an argument: the best arguments are ends in themselves, so it will not disappoint us if this one does not survive experience. It is true that posterity has done nothing for us and never will do anything. In point of fact (let us be candid) posterity is a nuisance—but, to be candid again, like many nuisances, we cannot do away with it; more—and this is the quintessence of the business—we cannot do without it. Only the suicide cuts posterity; but even then

RAMAKER LIBRARY
Northwestern College
Orange City, Iowa

posterity does not return the offensive : *noblesse
oblige.* Posterity, therefore, may be said to have
come to stop, and whatever attitude we adopt
towards it will make no difference either to it or to
ourselves. The days that are to come, with all their
folks and activities, their problems and adventures,
their teeming energies, joys and sorrows, stupidities and cupidities, splendours, meannesses and
trivialities, are more dominant in our lives than the
days that are gone, or even than those which are
still with us. The past influences us as openly
as the present. We yield graciously or un-
graciously according to temperament, disposition,
or whim. The upholders of tradition take the past
into partnership, just as modernists in art and life
declare war upon olden times.

But the influence of the future is insidious and
sly, making no fuss, demonstrating little, but
pulling, pulling all things, always, in the interests
of posterity. Nothing we do and nothing that
others do to us are unaffected by this prevailing
and powerful intrigue. Even any tendency to live
unreservedly and wholly in the present, which is
the aim of not a few, is curbed and guided by
Nature's regard for posterity. Life is always cast-

ing her bread upon the waters that she may receive it (with interest) after many days. And what life is doing in bulk we are repeating in detail, for are not we a part of life—" rolled round in earth's diurnal course, with rocks and stones and trees " ?

Whether we hate or love posterity, work for or against the future, is all one. Posterity will take toll of our little doings in this or any other present time. In this particular present time of grace, or the lack of it, posterity is having her will of us, and even winning advocates and proselytes of sorts. Some ninety years ago it was safe for Daniel Webster to comfort himself and others with the thought that " the past at least is secure." To-day he would have had to tune his hope to a different key. And although it may still be true, as was asserted many centuries ago, that even God is deprived of the power of eliminating the past, it is no longer true that the past can have all of its own way with us. Posterity is coming into its own—you can almost hear the future chuckling with satisfaction.

At one time indifference was the only enemy of the past, just as it was the only enemy of both the present and the future. But in such a kinetic age as ours even enmity towards what is almost a myth has become militant. Marinetti of Milan, and his brother Futurists, have thrown down the gage. They have declared war upon the past. · " Come, then, the good incendiaries with their charred fingers," cries he, " set fire to the shelves of the libraries ! Deviate the course of canals to flood the cellars of the museums ! Oh, may the glorious canvases drip helplessly ! Seize pickaxes and hammers ! Sap the foundations of the venerable cities ! " It is rhetorical, but it is war ; that is to say, war as the intellectual understands it— war of words. The Futurist poet is not going to do these brave things, he is only talking—but it shows the way the wind is blowing. The hour of posterity is at hand. And Nietzsche also was among the prophets, with his " Listen, ye lonely ones ! From the future winds are coming with a gentle beating of wings, and there cometh a good message for fine ears." What are these glad tidings for fine ears ? Hush, tell it not in Gath, for it may demoralize the underlings by puffing them out with undue and unwarrantable self-importance, for in very truth the thing that cometh is superman. Man is to be surpassed. Posterity is big with superman. Thus spake Zarathustra !

But why be so unscholarly as to buttress argument with modern instances ? Posterity has had propagandists from the days of Plato, and earlier ; to the days of William Morris, and later. So there may be something in it. The best evidence, however, is what is in yourself. The inward sense of responsibility towards posterity which we all feel at one time or another is a much greater reality than any reverence for the past. We all believe that we are going away from the past and getting nearer to the future. We are time-locked fore and aft. Our fathers are behind us, our children ahead. The spark of life is no *cul-de-lampe*, and we are right in honouring ourselves by fanning the flame of the future. " All this world is heavy with promise of greater things, and a day will come— one day in the unending succession of days—when beings, beings who are now latent in our thoughts and hidden in our loins, will stand upon this earth as one stands upon a footstool, and laugh and reach out their hands amidst the stars." The words are from H. G. Wells. They open vistas.

Posterity may have done precious little for us, but we must return good for ill, perforce ; for we ourselves are posterity to many pasts. But argument counts for little in such considerations. It is as well to regard the future intelligently and even generously, for, who knows, we may live long enough to need it ! At the same time we must not be over-zealous, for, who knows again, posterity may not agree with us, and it is far more comfortable to regret the good old times than to meet posterity half way.

ADVENTURES

for

R. A. FOSTER-
MELLIAR

*The plainest things are as obscure
as the most confessedly mysterious;
and the Plants we tread on are as
much above us as the Stars and
Heavens. The things that touch us
are as distant from us as the Pole ;
and we are as much strangers to
ourselves as to the inhabitants
of America.*—JOSEPH GLANVILL,
" Scepsis Scientifica " (1665).

WOODFIRES

You must gather the wood yourself, and saw and split it yourself . . . so let us begin at the beginning. . . . If you live in a town, which is more than likely, you are obviously at a disadvantage—your fireplace is probably of the wrong shape, and you are forced to the vulgar expedient of buying your wood. Bought wood is foreign to our purpose; there is a long story here which we shall not pursue, for it may lead us on to I know not what economic mysteries and anthropological entanglements; suffice it that bought wood is fallen wood, not wind-fallen, for that is not without advantage, as we shall see; it is wood with the bloom off even when it still wears its virginal bark—and that is insufferable. As for the more domesticated sorts of wood, often enough assembled in democratic bundles, or held together by oleaginous substances to trick the unwilling flame into life, such compromises are beneath us: what proper man would fall so low as to do aught but kindle a fire with the split infinitives of forgotten woodlands?

You should abstain also from unemployed packing-cases or superannuated sleepers, and all such man-handled scions of arboreal splendour; you must hitch your wagon to the stars of wood and dale; aspire to generous associations with lordly oak and elm and other fathers of the forest, whose aristocratic arms have known no master save the seasons, whose heads have bent only to the winds of heaven, whose grace and strength are born of immemorial freedoms, and whose bloom is the *patine* of the open air.

So let us have no traffic with the poor relations of the forest. Let the genealogy of our fuel be intact; its ancestry unambiguous. The proper fuel for town fires is coal or gas or electricity: compromise is pose.

All of which means that you must live near the wood as it grows, and you must sally forth with axe or saw, or failing that await the autumnal windfalls and frugally and reverently fold the fallen boughs as the shepherd folds his sheep. Happy he, be he so minded, if he live beside those friendly trees which do not scorn the habitations of man—ancestral elms, for instance, who in wrathful age scatter largesse of boughs as though anticipating your fireside needs. There are, I know, those writers on forestry who would have it that the elm is a treacherous fellow, but I prefer to believe that he is doing his best. True, he has a habit of throwing himself at you, but what of that ? Once you know his habit you can attend his robustious generosity from a safe distance. From such safe harbourage it is good to hearken to the ancient and upright fellows grinding their teeth against the equinoctial gales and crashing their boughs in the darkness of the night, for all terror is then merged in pleasurable anticipation of the harvest of the storm which you may hope to gather upon the shores of the morning.

A great storm in the second year of the war conquered many of our noblest and sturdiest trees, and in some southern counties sylvan giants lay prone and hapless across roads and meadows, like fallen warriors upon the battle-fields. It was sad to contemplate so much shattered loveliness— yet because fuel was scarce that year, and the winter interminable, we found refuge from sorrow at beauty in distress in the contemplation of so much profit for our hearths. We foregathered as for festival, like Esquimaux about a stranded school of whales! Town folk and suburbans long since civilized out of primitive activities leapt to attention at the command, so to speak, of the Gods of the Wild. Men, women, and children became woodfolk again as though by magic; and suburban lanes became animated idylls: scenes from *As You Like It.* You may be sure also that philosophic Jacques arose to point the moral and adorn the tale. The spirits that abide in woodfires renewed their acquaintance that year with those coal-burners long since marked among the lapsed and lost. But you need not wait upon windfalls such as these, nor upon the lesser windfalls of more familiar storms; these be happy accidents of fortune, and true thrift takes them in his stride as he sallies forth a-lumbering.

When your harvest is gathered and cut and stacked you may contemplate the dark days with fortitude. But before burning come the joys of cutting and splitting. If you can add to these the consciousness of having fallen your tree, then may you exult as a mighty hunter before the Lord. Such joy is not within the circle of my wood-faring.

I begin at the log, rolled on to my tiny demesne by greater brawn and skill than I possess. The big saw, rather than the adze, is my weapon. You lay him across your log, which has been nicely poised on a couple of smaller logs so that there can be no unequal pressure on him as his work proceeds. I say his work deferentially and deliberately, for your double-toothed saw goes about the business with the minimum of supervision. All you have to do is to place him squarely and swing him to and fro with a free rhythm and while you fall into a dream upon the generous patience of nature which has devoted some half a century to the up-rearing of so mighty a trunk for your fireside delight ; or maybe you sing. . . .

Then comes the process called splitting, and this is the manner of it : you throw your logs, cut some eight or ten inches thick, one at a time atop of a base log, and with a sharp knock of your sledge-hammer drive your first steel wedge into the outer rim. The blow should be so skilfully delivered that the wedge bites at once and forms a crack towards the centre into which you drive wedge number two with a swinging blow, which, if rightly delivered, severs the log in half. The process is repeated until your log is split into as many triangular sections as you require. It is an ancient game easily played, and its victories are measured by your own enjoyment and the extent of your growing wood-stack.

And when your logs are ablaze—your very own logs on your very own hearth—they do please you mightily, as Mr. Pepys would have said. How merrily they spurt and flare, as though congratulating themselves and you on this reunion, albeit it involves their own sacrifice. But it is a merrie end—a veritable dance of death—and in a good cause ! Is not cosiness a good cause ? Not, to be sure, as an end in life, but as an incident. We spend a third of our lives in bed ; a third in affairs, and a third, in winter at all events, sitting by fires. Did not man become man when he first learnt how to make wood burn ? All fires are friendly ; but the woodfire is the greatest friend —because it is the oldest. " Among so many things as are by men possessed or pursued in the course of their lives," said a king of Aragon, " all the rest are baubles besides old wood to burn, old wine to drink, old friends to converse with, and old books to read." Truly it is a woodfire sentiment. If Alphonsus had said " old coal to burn " the effect would not have been the same. Woodfires tell you things ; they gossip out of their endless memories, bridging the prepossessions and pursuits of man from the caves of the neolithic age to the villas of the age of devastation. And with their gossip is mingled the fragrance of the open air, distilled to its companionable essence—a woodland incense for the altar of cosiness ! And now, Reader, with your permission, I shall do homage before mine own example of that altar, learning thereby perchance a lesson in the greater luxury of warming both hands before the fire of life.

GARDENS OF DELIGHT

GARDENS of Epicurus—the poetry of gardens—where utility is forbidden unless she adapt herself to the needs of dalliance—are my theme. In the words of Sir Thomas Browne, I " pretend not to multiply vegetable divisions by quincuncial and reticulated plants ; or erect a new phytology," for that " field of knowledge hath been so traced," and " it is hard to spring anything new." Besides, has not necessity made good gardeners of us all ? That, however, is no reason why we should neglect our gardens of delight, for now is the heyday of the gardener, the old earth is beginning to reward him for his toil with many a green miracle, and once more we find our old love of gardens rekindling.

Yet garden-love is, perhaps, more rare in England than might at first be imagined. Our poets have sung of gardens, and our silent poets have enjoyed them, but I am forced into the belief that, strange as it may seem, there is more talk of gardening among those who are not poets than

about gardens. The majority of the lords of villas
in London and the provinces are for a short time,
or a long time, in the year devoted amateur
gardeners ; and a vast industry has come into
existence to meet their needs. Nurserymen, seeds-
men, toolmakers, authors, journalists, shop-
keepers, chemists, and a host of other obliging
people have joined in this amiable service. Yes,
the land is overflowing with gardening virtuosi.

Any night of any of the six working days at the
spring and summer seasons of the year you may
see innumerable representatives of the suburban
chivalry of England staggering homeward laden
with seeds and roots, insecticides and fertilizers,
trowels and sprayers and shears, and other
weapons used in the interminable war with Mother
Earth. And any Saturday afternoon or Sunday
morning you may hearken to the eternal *sizzle* of
the lawn-mower, or the rumble of the roller, or
the swift *yap-yap* of the shears ; and, peeping over
palings, you may observe hot, red faces with
beaded perspiration winking 'neath the brims of
old and battered hats, as their owners bend over
the rebellious old marl harrying grubs to their
doom, wreaking devastation among clamorous

115

weeds, or anxiously pouring destruction among invading hordes of green fly in the luxurious crowns of standard roses. After a while, should you be mean enough, or curious enough, to pursue your observations, you may note the owners of those faces in battered hats sink exhausted into canvas-hung deck-chairs, and, after toying limply with newspapers, depart swiftly into the realms of slumber, the while the beauties of the garden languish for lack of lovers.

I am not cynical about gardening; indeed, I have tried hard to appreciate, nay, practise the gentle craft; but, although it may be very wrong of me, I am entirely incapable of battering myself into any sort of enthusiasm for this heroic and disinterested activity. You see, I prefer gardens to gardening; and, though lacking enthusiasm, I am not without thankfulness and respect for those who make gardens. Without gardeners the gardens of the world would lose their savour. Nor am I against amateur gardeners; on the contrary, I honour them. But my own joy in gardening is made complete by the knowledge that somewhere in my garden, on certain days of the week, abides an observant, plodding yet leisurely, aged but happy man, bent and brown, and almost passive, mingling naturally alike with earth and growing things, from whose restful effort evolves order out of confusion ; from whose unobtrusive presence and slow laboriousness is created all the quiet loveliness of opulent border, rose-dowered pergola, and immortal English lawn.

But as I fall into a dream upon the beauty of such oases in life I am reminded of the ancient fact that the Book of Life began with a man and a woman in a garden, and I cannot but feel a kind of pity, unnecessary though that may be, that it should threaten to close with a perspiring business man under a battered hat chasing grubs. Gardeners, like poets, are born and not made, and those who are born to the craft never hurry, never seem to toil at all ; their work is a gentle growth, like the budding of a tree or the unfolding of a rose. Your amateur gardener is far too energetic ; he teases the garden and me. A garden should be reposeful :

A garden is a lovesome thing, God wot!
Rose plot, Fringed pool,
Fern'd grot—The veriest school
    Of peace. . . . .

117

the amateur gardener hurries, and Ruskin has reminded us that all haste is vulgar. Gardening is an art as well as a gift; in a wise society it might even become a religious function. But gardens themselves should always approximate to a gift, a gift of God, always made and never in the making—which is absurd, for we all know—but why labour that which we all know ? Let us proceed . . . .

Doubtless your amateur gardener has produced many pretty effects in the multitudinous patches of villa-burdened earth upon which he spends his leisure, but doubtless also he has rarely achieved that inevitability which is the final test of great art. A tour round the small gardens of a suburb confuses and distracts the mind. Suburban gardens are patchwork : they lack design in themselves and in the mass. That is a serious criticism, and seriously may I be called to book for making it. But I state a view of the matter, which is based on the conviction that no activity lends itself so readily to the practice of design as the creation of a garden out of wild nature. The essence of gardening should be design, and not, as so many people seem to imagine, the cultivation of as many plants as possible in a limited space.

Floriculture and gardening are as distinct as science and art. The things that grow are but the media of the gardener's art ; they should be no more to him than pigments are to the painter, or words to the writer, or marble to the sculptor. He should love his materials, as all artists do ; but the true gardener, taking his plot of earth as a painter takes his canvas, will, by the aid of certain instruments and certain potentially growing things, fashion a design which shall at once express him and them and contribute his joy to others. With trees and shrubs, with flowers and grass he should create rhythms of form and colour which should in turn not only appeal to our sense of form and our idea of beauty, but which should also minister to the native indolence of man. All of which means that the true gardener must be not merely a man of skill, but one well versed in the habits of growing things, deft in the use of his tools, and endowed also with the cunning of taste and the insight of imagination. Just such qualities as these are lacking in the majority of amateur gardeners. They have skill and knowledge and laboriousness, but, lacking vision, these are as nought.

Were it otherwise they would not rest with the monotony of suburban front and back gardens : they would demand a larger canvas, as it were, for their craft. Gardens are generally too small, and, above all, too private. There are, I know, excellent arguments for privacy in gardens, but privacy does not apply, except on special occasions, to the front gardens of villas and rows of houses. These are generally useless for any purpose save that of decoration. Such gardens ought to be treated in a public rather than a private spirit ; and the only way to do this is to throw a number of small gardens into one ; thus grouped together as an organic design in some sort of accord with the buildings and general surroundings. The weakness of the modern amateur garden is that it fails in relation to its attendant building; it lacks architectural balance. For, after all, a garden is a part of the house, and not a separate and independent thing. The design of a garden should repeat in its own convention, and with its own materials, the form and design of the building to which it belongs. That is half the secret of the beauty of many of the old gardens of English country houses, and of the formal gardens of Italy. Francis Bacon has it that "men come to build stately sooner than to garden finely; as if gardens were of the greater perfection." But men only come to garden finely when they have builded finely; and perhaps that is the crux of the matter. Our unimaginative small gardens may be the result of years of unimaginative building, but the renaissance of domestic architecture may liberate us from disproportionate and unseemly gardening. I do not doubt that once our amateur gardeners grasp the point all will be well, and the result of their endeavours will be things of beauty and joys for ever.

Meanwhile I shall not press the argument too far, for privacy, not alone in gardens, is among the virtues in a world given unduly unto prying and publicity.

SHIPS AND THE SEA

THE incredible events of the past years are having noticeable effect upon the minds of men. Among other things, our capacity for surprise is not what it was. Familiarity breeds, not contempt, but indifference. When the first German aeroplane hovered hawklike over Thanet one Christmas—or was it New Year's Day?—now so long ago, all Britain was staggered by the audacity of it; but when the Germans dropped their last bomb on London we had all settled down into a comfortable "things like this, you know, must be" sort of habit. Many of us just turned over and went to sleep again. Even more surprising things leave us cold in these even more amazing days of "Peace." Not an eyebrow is raised by the news that Nelson's *Victory* is disintegrating through old age and will presently sink in Portsmouth Harbour unless something is done to save her. No one turns a hair at the proposed destruction of the super-Dreadnoughts which have succeeded the *Victory*. We are a ship-

fed people. The sea is in our blood. The beauty
of ships and the mystery of the sea are the pillars
of our romance. Yet we do not wonder at this
twilight of the seagods.

Is there a heart so tame that has not beaten
quicker at thought or sight of ships ? Is there a
boy of us who has not, at least for one wild moment,
listened rapturously to the syren song of the sea
and felt joy at the glimpse of a spar ; anon to walk
in high dudgeon because of the parental tyranny
which thwarted ambition to emulate Drake and
Nelson or, perhaps, Paul Jones or Captain Hook ?

We have all dreamed these piratical dreams, and
most of us, alas, have awakened to the comfortable
realities of the life of the land-lubber. O we of
little faith ! For no nobler pirates ever lived than
we were, in our dreams—nor was Nelson greater
than we were then. Because we had not the
courage of our dreamland convictions we were
doomed to a life ashore. Doomed ! Why doomed ?
Immaculate reader, we are sentimentalizing. We
are allowing our emotions to run away with our
pen. " Doomed " to a life ashore, forsooth ! and
what is wrong with that life, pray ? Can we not
read of ships in books and see them from a safe

distance ? The joy we have in them is still vouch-
safed to us, and when vacation time comes round
we journey to coastwise towns, where from cliff
or beach or promenade we gaze wistfully at the
sailing of the inshore boats, or feed romantic
desire upon a binocular vision of the deep-sea
craft beyond the range of ordinary sight.

The fascination of ships is not, however, merely
romantic. The beauty of ships is as real as the
beauty of the sea. Ships are our good and
immemorial allies, therefore do we love them.
But their beauty is so marked that did we hail
from regions remote from all great waters we must
needs come under the spell of such grace at once.
The beauty of a ship is irresistible ; it commands
us instantly, like Nature in her great moments—
like St. Paul's Cathedral from Fleet Street—like
Bath, or Oxford, or Cambridge—like Queen
Anne's Gate—like Gwydyr House. . . .

The reason . . . but is it not obvious, this
beauty of ships ? Is not a ship a cosmos, an
inevitable arrangement, a complete adaptation of
materials to purpose and condition ? Ships are
works of art. This readiness to scrap the past and
wed the present, this off with the old and on with

the new fickleness, has made the ship a thing of
beauty down the ages. It made the ship as beautiful in those early days when Briton made futile
effort with his coracle against the galleons of
Rome as it was in the days when Nelson sailed the
Sound, or Beatty the Bight of Heligoland ; when
the *Golden Hind* put out from Plymouth or the
Mauretania left Liverpool.

The beauty of ships is no idle sentiment, no
romantic fancy ; it is very real : inevitable as
wind and wave. To the wind and the sea we must
turn to solve the mystery. The beauty of ships is
born of a treaty between wind and sea. The ship
herself is born of these and largely subject to their
moods, yet is she autonomous by virtue of her
recognition of the irrefutable law by which the
elements abide and by the way she has adapted
herself to them.

The idea of the ship is embodied in her form,
a form which must remain until there is no more
sea. And when the mariner goes forth into deep
waters, where there is no guidance save the stars
and the magnetic needle, fear has no place in his
heart, for he is protected by the design of his
craft ; he knows how strong her beauty is and how

sure her form. And he knows also that his own seamanship is bone of her bone and flesh of her flesh, in that he rules by obedience to the same laws which gave her being. Even in that ill hour when wind and wave conspire to hurl him to destruction he does not blame the good ship as she trembles upon the reef, later maybe to strew the beach with silent wreckage. He faces the fact calmly, as brave men face death. Complaint is useless. She was a good ship all the same.

Neither is it fantastic to imagine the sea not tolerating any form that lacks this perfection of design. All sea things are beautiful, as the ship is beautiful; where there is ungainliness it is due to a compromise with the land. Most amphibious animals are ugly compared with the grace and balance of aquatic creatures. That which seeks the sea in aught but the strength of perfect line and form courts destruction. The ugliest ships have been failures—the *Great Eastern*, built for the Atlantic ferry service, was more of a tank than a ship, and she became a cable tank, and ultimately a coal hulk. Her ugliness was her doom ; and so it was with the early paddle-steamers, which were just plodding their way to grace. Ungainly rafts may be immune from peril on river or lagoon, but they must not aspire to the sea until they have found grace.

So it is that every proper raft dreams of the day on which she shall become even as the queens of the merchant service—figuring, no doubt, the evolution from the humble coracle through sampan and canoe, link by link, until the alliance with the chosen of the mighty deep is attained. It is not the mere fact of floating that makes an object acceptable to the sea. The adjustment of this primary faculty to the conditions of ebb and flow, of wind and wave, must be perfectly carried out before any negotiations are possible. When these are complete the beauty of the ship is also complete. Then wood and steel have become strong in grace, symbols of the skilled intelligence of ship-craft, urged into being by imagination and judgment. Then only are they sent forth with the title " seaworthy " in deference to the might of Neptune.

The old romance of ships has gone, because those old days of the sea, when ships went forth pranked with images of gold upon their prows and gorgeous heraldry astern, and vast sails brave with rich dyes, worthy harness for the winds of heaven, are no more. Here and there, robbed of their ancient glory, these dandies of the deep do service yet as training ships. The old beauty is still upon them as they doze in quiet harbours—ponderous masses haunted by ancient memories, dreaming, no doubt, of Copenhagen and the Nile and the days of the sea kings.

But instead of the old romance we have the new. It is no longer called romance ; no longer are ships decked in the trappings of the joy of life ; the lines of our modern ships are beautiful with a beauty strange to that of other days. The line is different, it is sterner and sharper, more masculine ; the shipwright has not stopped to glorify his skill with bright colours or rich carvings. He has pared away all that does not serve his aim, for his aim is speed. He has created a new beauty and a new romance, and the beauty is called utility and the romance reality.

We harness the winds less and less. No longer do we tack and tack obediently to the demand of the Valkyries. A new power urges our ships independently of wind and tide. With the growth of steam power the crowning glory of the old ship departed. Masts, with their intricate rigging, have shrunk as funnels have grown in size and numbers. Ships have suffered a sea-change into something rich and strange, but the spirits of steam and the gods of speed have recreated their eternal beauty—the beauty of the machine.

INSTEAD OF A SPRING SONG

For, lo, the winter is past, the rain is over and gone; the flowers appear on the earth ; the time of the singing of birds is come, and the voice of the turtle is heard in our land. . . .

Sometimes the happiest of us feel that life is of little value in this workaday world. The sun shines, and we go on working ; winds shout, birds sing ; memories of coloured cities in brighter climates invite us, and the rolling, bare-backed downs beckon—but all for nothing ; we go on working. We go on working, most of us, merely for daily bread, and the remainder from habit, from ineptitude, or—to encourage the others. But we have to nudge each other to remind ourselves that we like it, for all that ; and when the springfret comes we know we don't! I should like to write about the springfret, but no one would thank me if I did ; few have understanding of such things, and I am not one of those who write to give people understanding : I write for those who

have it. I do not think you can give people anything worth having ; we, all of us, have the real
things within us, if we only knew it, and the
springfret is one of them.

It comes on one day of the year, in the morning,
generally on the first morning of spring. I do not
mean on March 21. That need not necessarily be
the first day of spring. The first day of spring is
the first day after the winter on which the sun
lights up ; the day on which you are brought face
to face again with the facts of light—when a white
door becomes opalescent, when the dull buds of
the hawthorn twinkle into stars of green fire, when
the leafless plane-trees waken into shadowy green
and grey traceries. Then beware, or, if you are
fearless, be glad, for the springfret may be on you
at any moment, and during its continuance you are
not worth your salt in places where men buy and
sell.

But, in spite of that, the merchandise of it is
better than the merchandise of silver and the gain
thereof than fine gold. It is the invitation of the
sun, it is the whisper of the wild, bidding you lay
down your tools and your nets and follow, follow,
you know not whither, for man knows not what is

good or bad for him. You only know that when the white door becomes opalescent, and the hawthorn buds green fire, you suffer a kind of nausea in the face of all humdrum things and long to have done with them, to break free, to run wild for a time. And why should you not ? For you do not ; you simply fight it down, like the good sensible fellow you are. You fight it down and plunge into the brown air of commerce again, until next year. It is always next year, " always jam to-morrow," as Alice said, " but never jam to-day," and when the same old spur to rebellion comes at you again —once more you force it from you, for next year, like to-morrow, never comes. But the day will come when the light will shine full on common things, giving them distinction, and you will see it not. In that hour the springfret will pass you by. " The grasshopper shall be a burden, and desire shall fail . . ." You may look through your office window at the blue sky interlaced with telephone cables, and yearn for Saskatchewan, or shake your fist at the engine on Ludgate Bridge, protesting your determination to fly to the South Seas. You will be too old.

That is life's tragedy—to find suddenly that you

are too old ; to find that you no longer desire to play truant, that you are become a mere Mantalini doomed to know only that " life is nothing but one demnition grind," even when the spring comes in, and the sun wakes up, and the Strand and Cheapside become temples of light ; to find that you are good for nothing but to stay at home and be good. I suppose that is the fate of most of us, and, perhaps, we deserve it. Well, well, let me be generous, and say we do ; for if we did otherwise deserve, and answered not the promptings of the springfret, then I should have to say a worse thing.

It is not good at all times to ride our souls on the curb. We should give them their heads when they seem to need it—that is, when the need becomes sufficiently dominant. Needs are made to be gratified, even if they are only whims. Let us not be supercilious about whims like the springfret, for it is Nature's summons to growth. It is the old Divine frenzy of life working within us, urging us to slough our habits as the snake casts his skin. Let us answer in the same spirit.

" That," I fancy I hear you say, " is all very well, but what shall we do ; how can we answer

133

in the same spirit ? " And there, if I may say it,
you have me. I did not set out to tell you how to
answer the springfret, because I don't know. I
know, to be sure, how I shall answer it, or, rather,
how I have answered it after I have done so ;
and I know also how my friend will answer it, the
friend who babbled o' sunny climes and eternal
afternoons of loafing, the while he fed himself with
chump chop and *pommes sautées* ; but as for you,
dear reader, to tell you the truth, you have the
advantage of me. I sympathize with you, but
I know you not. Were it otherwise, I doubt if I
could be of much use, because each of us answers
the springfret in his own way. Should you be
young and at school you play truant, and take the
ultimate thwackings at the appointed hour (for
there is always an appointed hour) without regret.
Are you a little older (or much older, as the case
may be), you fall in love—you know the poetics
of it : " In the spring the young man's fancy
lightly turns to thoughts of love "—and there are
worse eventualities ; but let us not waste time and
space on what is obvious. Then, if you are of no
particular age, but just on the right side of being
alive, you—well, there it is, no one can say of a

certainty what you will do, but you will of a certainty do it. You will, in short, let the spring-fret have its way with you, even if you lose money in the transaction.

All this may sound nonsense, and I am not one of those who would for a moment suggest another name for it. Nonsense it may be, and nonsense we shall let it be ; but is it any the worse for that ? The sensible things to do are associated with keeping yourself in hand, well in hand for the matter of that ; and, when the spring urges, not to throw down your tools has been the method and habit of all sensible folk from time immemorial. But the foolish ones have done otherwise. They have yielded to the springfret, and at the end of the day's march they have laughed quietly to themselves, quietly and gladly, at the thought of the rebel days, and they have gone hence murmuring to their consciences that, in spite of all and after all, it has been somehow good : life has been spent. As for the others at the same lone hour, they also say things to themselves, but the things they say are far different. They say, Alas, how good it might have been ! But I must not end on so sad a note, for, after all, we are not dead yet.

Not dead yet, did I say ? I must be careful, for
one never knows about such things. Life and
death are debatable. It is not only the dead who
are dead ; the living are often in the same sad
plight. Indeed, there are evidences to prove that
the dead are not so dead as those who imagine
they know would have us believe. And when I
look about me, and take stock, as it were, of my
fellow-men, I am often moved by the reflection
that all is not well with them (or me, for the matter
of that), that, in short, they are not quite so much
alive as they think they are. The attitude towards
the springfret is the real test ; it tells us who's who
more vividly than any stout year-book of cele-
brities. You just want to watch people under the
thrall of the thing, and, watching carefully, you
may note differences. You may realize, in fact,
that the laughter and the light of things are
tangled with the peculiar restlessness which comes
upon men and animals at the springtime of the
year. And now, I fancy, I must close as rapidly
as may be, or there is danger of these words lapsing
into moral reflections, which would be absurd.
Moral concepts and the springfret have nothing
in common. At the same time, the springfret and

morals have no particular enmity—their quarrel is too ancient for that. They have long since grown to ignore each other, and will continue so to do until one or the other passes hence.

SOMEWHERE IN NOWHERE

EVEN the determined pessimist who has so little faith in humanity as to rely entirely upon the driving power of force is convinced that if you hammer an enemy hard enough you will eventually hammer him into a better neighbour. The persistence of this uncanny faith in spite of the evidence of history, and in the face of Christian teaching, proves not the power of force but the power of illusion. We cling to our illusions as if they were our most precious possessions—perhaps they are. Perhaps life itself is the supreme illusion, mastering all, eternally teasing us out of consciousness of the ultimate reality behind and within all things. This may explain the poets and them that see visions and dream dreams. It also may explain the average man who physics himself with hope against disillusion. Not for nothing are our popular sentimental songs Utopist. " There's a Good Time coming, Boys—so wait a little longer," of yesterday, and " Somewhere the Stars are Shining," of to-day, are equally criticisms of

138

life with *Rabbi Ben Ezra* and *Prometheus Unbound*.
But though the pain of living may be narcotized
by hope, life is not helped thereby. Unless we
either permit ourselves to flow with the stream
towards the better land of our dreams, or, better
still, unless we are willing to make some effort to
speed up the sailing thither, we are little more than
sentimentalists, treacherous alike to the present
and the future.

At this hour,[1] more than any other hour in the
history of the world, " the kingdom of heaven
suffereth violence," we are all actors in a tragic
drama which had a sudden beginning but has no
apparent end. But Somewhere in the Nowhere of
the sphinx-like future an end is in the making.
For the man of goodwill it matters less when it
will be than what it will be. This last thought has
filled the world with a new hope which many
believe to be realizable, in spite of the fact that no
one has yet arisen with sufficient imagination to
give it form and direction. The talk is still of
Freedom, Democracy, and Peace, just as during
the last European upheaval the talk was of

[1] December 1917; the essay appeared in *To-day,* January
1918.

Liberty, Equality, and Fraternity. For a hundred years social philosophers have been trying to give practical definition to the slogan of the French Revolution—and Liberty, Equality, and Fraternity are still homeless words with many lip-servants, with none so true of heart and sure of conviction as to do them practical reverence. Will Freedom, Democracy, and Peace share the same fate ?

They are in danger of doing so unless we cease to look upon them as the mere spoils of conquest. The renaissance of hope is the child of tragedy, and it looks beyond and above victory for fulfilment. It is beginning to dawn upon the world that conquest achieves little ; the thing that purifies and strengthens is the good fight, not the final victory. The evil genius of all romantic adventure is the conqueror ; the good genius is the fighter who is prepared to take great risks in a noble cause regardless of the end. Defeat in a good cause is better than victory in a bad one. But what the world needs to-day is a victory over conquest ; if the present tragedy could achieve such a victory, if we could see conquest " dragged captive through the deep," then might we speedily anticipate good news from the Nowhere of our dreams.

We are not likely to get this news from those who shout loudest, for they make so much noise that they could not hear the glad tidings, and worse, their noise would prevent others from hearing. But that Somewhere in Nowhere is speaking to the present. Its winged message is inspiring the new hope which is the first step towards the creation of a new will to life, resplendent and full, not necessarily secure and peaceful—security and peace are barren things, but rich with the promise of splendid activities and more wonderful adventures than any yet recorded in story or song. The gospel of Nowhere is not unwritten. Every dreamer who has put his dreams into words has recorded some of its news. But none of our poets has imagined a morality more useful to the present hour than Shelley. It is he who has uttered the most inspiring Utopian thought in the noblest form ; and of all his magical words those which conclude *Prometheus Unbound* are of more value to us in this dark hour before the dawn than any other words in our own or any other language. Could we forget everything

else and learn their full meaning we should save
the world :

Gentleness, Virtue, Wisdom, and Endurance,
These are the seals of that most firm assurance
    Which bars the pit over Destruction's strength;
And if, with infirm hand, Eternity,
Mother of many acts and hours, should free
    The serpent that would clasp her with his
        length ;
These are the spells by which to reassume
An empire o'er the disentangled doom.

To suffer woes which Hope thinks infinite ;
To forgive wrongs darker than death or night;
    To defy Power, which seems omnipotent;
To love, and bear; to hope till Hope creates
From its own wreck the thing it contemplates;
    Neither to change, nor falter, nor repent;
This, like thy glory, Titan, is to be
Good, great and joyous, beautiful and free ;
This is alone Life, Joy, Empire, and Victory.

The path to such an ideal may be beset with
many difficulties, but what of that ? Great souls
reject the easy way. Somewhere in Nowhere such

politics as Shelley's are practicable, and they are the more alluring because they do not depend upon others. They need no advocacy; they can be begun at home. To practise them you have not to extend your national boundaries or defend or subjugate other peoples. To practise them you have to invade yourself. Utopia is not the country you are going to enter to-morrow; it is a country you can enter to-day. Shelley was expelled from Oxford for atheism, just as Jesus was crucified outside Jerusalem for heresy, but both Shelley and Jesus asserted that the Kingdom of God was within, and that you could best open it to others by first entering it yourself.

ON LOSING ONESELF

THERE are very few of us who want to lose ourselves for ever, but most of us have desired to get lost at one time or another, if only for a change. Some have had the courage to try, others have done so by accident. It is a risk most fear whilst craving to take it, and only the peculiarly constituted take and chance it. Yet impulse ever bids us " make tracks into the unknown," leave the beaten paths with their stale familiarities and acquaint ourselves with strangeness. From childhood upward there would seem to be a kindly conspiracy against any tendency to lose ourselves. Our earliest fears are of getting lost. We are only permitted to toddle within call at the beginning of our days, and we only permit ourselves to totter within call at the close. And when the end of all draws nearer still our fear is of the strangeness that may follow. Shall we emerge into some familiar dream-realm of bliss ? Will the God we have learned to know through faith or worship welcome us on the threshold . . . or

some unknown God in an uncharted Heaven ?
But more fearful is the feeling that we cannot get
back. It is the child's fear of getting lost, and to
combat it we have sought out many inventions for
our consolation. We have plunged into spiritual
ecstasies for companionship—peopled the astral
world with friendly souls who are neither dead nor
sleeping, but ever wakeful and alert for opportunities to reassure us that far from having gone
hence they are here among us now—eternally at
home ! When a baby of Japan smiles in its sleep
its parents believe it to be in communion with the
happy dead ; but the smiles of a sleeping English
baby are still attributed to indigestion.

All of which does not destroy the fascination of
losing oneself. Perhaps it increases it. You may
learn something by getting lost. A child will risk
getting lost out of curiosity or from sheer impishness. Mark some infant voyager among the
domestic archipelagos of the larger furniture.
How gingerly he takes his compassless way—
surprised at his successful doubling of the vast
Chesterfield reef, and tearful though undaunted
by his collision with the coal-scuttle, until at length
the still lagoon beneath the shade of the dining

table is reached, where he may map out the return journey in comparative safety. Stage by stage his growth is marked by ever-widening circles of adventure and more splendid successions of chance, until he learns the great lesson that it is only by risking loss that you learn to find.

Then comes manhood with its unblushing certainties, and unless he has inherited or contracted the divine restlessness of a Cabot or a Cook he will settle down within a prescribed area, ferrying safely between office and home until he crosses the bar under sealed orders.

It is curious that at most times in our lives we should court the things we dread; but a mysterious fate has made this inclination one of the most common of human characteristics. It is a peculiarity we share with the bewitched mouse who, instead of retreating precipitately from the environment of his feline enemy, returns again and again as though infatuated by the jaws of death. So folks who dwell on the slopes of volcanic mountains return and rebuild their homes after each eruption. For centuries Vesuvius and Cotopaxi have revolted against human ideals of peace and order without succeeding in scaring away men and women who presumably have no wish for premature death in spite of appearances to the contrary. And so also, as criminal investigation proves, the malefactor returns to the scene of his crime, regardless of the dangers of apprehension which he is fully aware must threaten such a proceeding. This flirtation with the red eyes of danger must not be mistaken for heroic courage. Its cause must be sought elsewhere. Courage will risk losses of all kinds, including the loss of liberty and consciousness ; but those who wish to get lost for no particular or easily discoverable reason are as children who play with fire, or like the member of the Suicide Club in Robert Louis Stevenson's story who risked compulsory suicide for the subtle joy of frightening himself, but when he drew the fatal lot which earmarked him for immediate annihilation his interest in death changed to an even more extravagant interest in life.

From this it might be argued that if loss were certain no one but a crank or a lunatic would want to lose himself—but nothing is certain in this world—not even death. That is the secret of life's charm and tragedy. When Socrates met his death with that cheerfulness which marked him out from

147

all men, Crito inquired on behalf of his friends,
who dreaded losing the philosopher: " How shall
we bury you?" And Socrates made his famous
answer: "As you please—only, you must catch me
first." Even Socrates glamoured the most noble of
deaths with the idea of chance, as though realizing
in spite of his own splendid certainty that, as
Anatole France pointed out two thousand years
afterwards, chance in the last resort was God.

The implication is not that they that take
chances seek God, but that God determines the
chance that they take and thus dominates the
game of life—the spirit of play. It is the idea
behind all scepticism: from Lucretius to the author
of the *Garden of Epicurus*, from Omar Khayyam
to—Edward FitzGerald:

But helpless Pieces of the Game He plays
Upon his Chequer-board of Nights and Days;
Hither and thither moves, and checks, and slays,
And one by one back in the Closet lays.

The Ball no question makes of Ayes and Noes,
But Here or There as strikes the Player goes;
And He that tossed you down into the Field,
He knows about it all—He knows—HE knows.

Perhaps, by some subliminal hope deep down in our hearts, we are impelled to the belief, scarcely intelligible even to ourselves, that by getting lost we cheat Fate for a brief spell.

Yet the matter may have a very much more simple solution than any we have considered. The fascination of getting lost may after all be no more than an instinctive offensive against boredom. Losing ourselves is running away from ourselves. One of the many " movements " of our time concerned itself with self-expression. It was a superfluous little movement, but great fun whilst it lasted. Ibsen was elected high-priest (much to the amiable playwright's surprise), and later Nietzsche's philosophy was requisitioned as a stimulant. Devotees went about nudging themselves and each other to be themselves, with the curious result that they became each other so effectively that they could only remember they were themselves at all by wearing green or red ties and dilapidated hats. Their liveliest fulminations were against boredom and seriousness, and there were no more bored people in the whole world than they, and none more serious.

Throughout all life boredom like a green-eyed

monster has lurked in the background of our bliss; but none are so bored as those who are unduly interested in themselves. The burden of self is the modern evil; few escape it, and many of our recreations, so appropriately called " distractions " and " pastimes," are vain attempts to lighten the burden. We actually hear people saying, " I must get away from myself for a while," and at certain times of the year everybody is dealing in the current platitudes about holidays not being necessary solely on physical grounds but on psychological grounds as well. We do not only want change of air, they say, but change of scene and company. In short, they want, in a limited sense, to lose themselves. All respite from the necessary but ultimately tedious insistences of life is akin to losing oneself. One casts oneself upon the waters of Lethe, as it were, that one may receive oneself after many days cleaned of world-weariness. . . . and so whether we fly from dullness " charioted by Bacchus and his pards " or " on the viewless wings of poesy " we indulge in the pleasing process of getting lost as a medicine for the soul. True health, however, requires no physic—but that is another argument.

TALKING ABOUT THE WEATHER

WHEN the Lords of Sun and Wind and Cloud have been more than usually capricious, as they are very often, to talk about the weather is permissible. The best people do it—they who sit in the front seats of Olympus wagging tongues about that only which is high and authoritative and remote. In some circumstances everybody does it : superior and inferior alike, everybody does it openly and without apology ; at other times and in other circumstances superior people discuss the weather guiltily, with a sense of sin, fearing to be thought commonplace. They miss much, those fearful ones, for the weather is a very proper topic : a topic of incalculable variety, immemorial usage, exalted authority, and infinite jest. We have, in fact, discussed the weather for so many generations that the subject has become the raw material of national small-talk and not a little of our art.

It is easier to sneer at small-talk than to explain

TALKING ABOUT THE WEATHER

it away. Small-talk is a social necessity, if only because it helps to bridge the gaps between thought and thought, and silence and silence. But it does more than that. Small-talk may be the noise made by the human rattle, but it is also one of the disguises of the thoughtful . . . and the cunning. But talk about the weather is not always small-talk in an eccentric climate like ours ; it is very often the one topic of enthralling interest.

How soon do we tire of other topics : politics, one's back garden, race-suicide, the latest novel, the newest art, one's ailments, one's servants, that cat Mrs. de Jones-Brown, or that cad Smith-Robinson, or the latest in hats ! But the weather as a conversational subject is eternal ; it is our national topic. Other topics rise and fall like stocks and shares in Throgmorton Street ; they have their brief spells of activity and pass away ; but the weather is always with us—most threadbare of subjects, battered and frayed and torn, lacking honour among topics ; treated with contempt and exercised with apologies, it, nevertheless, holds its own, coming up smiling after every taunt and rebuff and ill-usage : an incontestable example of the survival of the fittest. Even politics, the one topic which, by reason of its futility and inconclusiveness, runs the weather very closely, takes a second place. Indeed, politics, like religion, are *taboo* in polite circles—except at political breakfasts, which the best people no longer attend. Nowadays we do not discuss politics ; we sneer at them. We do not even discuss new Acts of Parliament ; we discuss ways and means of evading them.

Even the War, which destroyed so many ideas and made so many topics obsolete, has left the weather topic unscathed. We still discuss the weather. No longer do we inquire eagerly after each other's health, and " How do you do ? " is a form of greeting surviving only among the *nouveaux riches*. Now and then, to be sure, Dame Nature or the newspapers may distract us with pyrotechnics, but, let them be never so captivating, they cannot decoy us far or for long from the true faith. We always return to the weather. It is our topical anchorage ; the sanctuary of the short of speech ; the scratching-post of small-talk. When we British discuss the weather we purr.

One might be disposed in one's enthusiasm to conclude that so great a subject needed no advocacy: it has survived the War—it will survive anything. True : but there are, as we have seen, ill-disposed persons, clever folk, barren of goodwill, who for the sake of cleverness would rob us of our topical birthright. True, also, they have proved impotent ; but to be forewarned is to be fore-armed. We must not sell our birthright for a mess of brilliance. It is good, therefore, to know that the great topic is championed by that watch-dog of our traditions the University of Oxford. There, where our " young barbarians " used to play, at the Clarendon Press thereof, which in all probability they regarded not, the national topic has been enshrined delectably in the most enduring of monuments.[1] It is a little book, but as big with eternity as its subject, and within its quaintly-marbled covers, as variably grained as its theme, the testimonies of certain impenitents are set forth in such manner as to justify all and sundry henceforth in their predilection for this topic. It adds to common usage the sanction of distinguished precedent with the imprimatur of Oxford—now at

[1] *The Weather Calendar, or a Record of the Weather for Every Day in the Year.* Being a Series of Passages collected from Letters and Diaries, and arranged by Mrs. Henry Head.

length, and henceforth, no longer, " home of lost causes," for she has allied herself with the un-losable. From John Stow to Edward FitzGerald the chroniclers, diarists, and gossips produce their evidence, evidence of four hundred years, and, even then, incomplete; but, were all the æons trawled, bulk alone would be increased, not evidence, for that is complete. The evidence proves more than the permanence of the topic, it estab-lishes its distinction, and provides us with the data of an interest which needed no proving. References to the weather would seem to indicate the existence of two very admirable qualities— goodwill and wonder. When men who pass in the street salute each other with a hurried "It's a fine day!" or its contrary, it is not out of idleness or shortage of ideas ; it is merely a short way, suit-able to the occasion, of saying, " God be with you, sir ! On such a glorious and invigorating day as this it is more than good to be alive ! " If the contrary, say, " Filthy weather ! " it is an intima-tion of the desire for communal disgruntlement, " let us talk of graves " as it were ; sympathy in sorrow, the *camaraderie* of gloom. Such senti-ments can no more be dull than they can grow old.

155

They are the vocal symbols of goodwill, the sounds of sociability.

As to the wonder, is it not the key of our happiness, the corner-stone of our romance ? Without wonder we should scarcely live, and without the weather we should rarely wonder. Proof ? Look at the races of man ; has ever an equable climate produced an active or an imaginative race ? It is equable in the Arctic zone, but does poetry or progress flourish among the Esquimaux ? It is equable in Sahara—what then ? In England the weather is so variable that every morning brings a renascence of wonder and every night the possibility of climatic adventure ; and in this land of meteorological inventiveness has grown up the most acquisitive and imaginative people in the world. The English people have achieved the two most amazing things in history—they have given to the world Industrialism and Shakespeare, and, probably, they would have done neither if their interests and enthusiasms, their sense of wonder had not been sharpened by a climate which made the weather of such infinite variety that the national mind is kept from rusting by the mere contemplation of it.

No matter what pranks our weather plays we never cease to wonder. " The weather is very odd this year," wrote Mrs. Piozzi, in March 1804 ; was the weather ever otherwise in March, or at any other season ? Yet Mrs. Piozzi wondered. Horace Walpole rebelled against the wet June of 1768 : " In short, every summer one lives in a state of mutiny and murmur," why ?—" Because we will affect to have a summer, and we have no title to any such thing." This same Walpole records, with equal surprise, a December, twenty years earlier, so "entirely free from frosts" that honeysuckles and nectarines blossomed in the open ; and the weather impressionist records an equally paradoxical day on July 1, 1789, when the weather tolerated all " winter diversions," which led him to confess that it struck him " thirty years ago that this is the most beautiful country when framed and glazed, that is, when you look through a window with a good fire behind you." And so they, and we, go on wondering at every change, surprised by every sameness ; convinced that the seasons are not as they used to be, and that the " old-fashioned winter " is a thing of the past, that a hard winter means a fine summer and *vice*

157

versa ; and finally and always forgetting Wordsworth's familiar dictum, that the weather is never
so bad as it appears to be when viewed through a
parlour window. . . .

But the topic is not monopolized by the small-
talkers ; it is a very real asset of our poets, and,
from the days of Turner and Constable, of our
best and worst painters. The poets have made it
peculiarly their own. With that inspired sense of
fact which is one of the chief qualities of your poet,
they have recognized, with more ordinary people,
that the English climate is a masterly series of
quick changes ; but, unlike the ordinary person,
they have also recognized that these quick climatic
variations are infinitely charming and brimful of
interest and delight. The use of the weather in
English nature-poetry is the secret of much of its
beauty and fascination, and English nature-poetry
is the best in the world. " Shall I compare thee to
a summer's day ? " asked Shakespeare, when he
wished to pay a compliment, and when he sang
to charm one with the idea of a woodland life he
said : " There shall he find no enemy but winter
and rough weather." Throughout the whole of
English poetry you will find this recognition of the

158

importance of the weather. The weather is the hero of our national poetry. The changes of the seasons, fair days and dull days, heat and cold, skies of cloud and skies of deepest blue, storm and calm, rain and wind and snow—these are much more the materials of our lyric poets than any images of Sherwood and its merrie men, Tintagel or Glastonbury and their pale knights, or " all Olympus' faded hierarchy."

I should not like to say how much of English poetry reflects the effect of the weather upon temperament, but it must be very considerable. That is only natural, for we are to a large extent creatures of the weather ; the weather affects us in its infinite variations, and, if it affects ordinary folk like ourselves, how much more should it affect our poets, who are the highly-sensitized and impressionable echoes of ourselves. The greatest of our poets—Shakespeare, Keats, Shelley, Words-worth—are never tired of discussing the weather ; they find the subject enthralling. Can one ever forget Lear's apostrophe ?—

Poor naked wretches, wheresoe'er you are,
That bide the pelting of this pitiless storm,

How shall your houseless heads and unfed sides,
Your loop'd and window'd raggedness, defend you
From seasons such as these ? O I have ta'en
Too little care of this ! Take physic, pomp;
Expose thyself to feel what wretches feel,
That thou mayst shake the superflux to them
And show the heavens more just . . . .

Or how the weather clothes the naked majesty of that great tragedy? It is one of the great charms of Keats that he is able to make the weather the keynote to so many of his poems ; how superbly does he do this in the opening to " The Eve of St. Agnes "—

St. Agnes' Eve—Ah, bitter chill it was!
The owl, for all his feathers, was a-cold;
The hare limp'd trembling through the frozen
 grass,
And silent was the flock in woolly fold:
Numb were the Beadsman's fingers, while he told
His rosary, and while his frosted breath,
Like pious incense from a censer old,
Seem'd taking flight for heaven, without a death,
Past the sweet Virgin's picture, while his prayers
 he saith.

160

And Shelley bathes his passionate song in atmospheric effects, rising to magical heights in the " Ode to the West Wind "—

> *Thou on whose stream,'mid the steep sky's commo-*
> > *tion,*
> > *Loose clouds like earth's decaying leaves are*
> > *shed,*
> *Shook from the tangled boughs of Heaven and Ocean,*
> > *Angels of rain and lightning : there are spread*
> *On the blue surface of thine airy surge,*
> > *Like the bright hair uplifted from the head*
> *Of some fierce Mænad, even from the dim verge*
> > *Of the horizon to the zenith's height*
> *The locks of the approaching storm. Thou dirge*
> > *Of the dying year, to which this closing night*
> *Will be the dome of a vast sepulchre,*
> > *Vaulted with all thy congregated might*
> *Of vapours, from whose solid atmosphere*
> > *Black rain, and fire, and hail will burst : Oh*
> > *hear!*

Wordsworth depends so much upon the changes in the weather that I could fill pages with examples : Wordsworth is more than a Lake Poet —he is a Weather Poet. His very praises of women and children are atmospheric : " Three years she grew in sun and shower," and " The floating clouds their state shall lend her." And could the immortal lines,

> *Fair as a star, when only one*
> *Is shining in the sky,*

have been written by a poet living under less mutable skies than ours ? Whilst the weather plays a subtle part in the great sonnets composed upon the beach near Calais and upon Westminster Bridge.

It is not necessary to continue these excerpts from the poets ; they abound for all who desire to follow the idea further. The essence of the matter is that to despise those who discuss the weather is no sign of superiority. The weather can be an entrancing as well as a proper topic.

BOOKS

for

JAMES LEWIS
MAY

Time captivated and snatched from thee by incursions of business, thefts of visitants, or by thy own carelessness lost, is by these redeemed in life ; they are the soul's viaticum ; and against death its cordial.—BULSTRODE WHITELOCKE (1605-1675).

BOOKMEN

THIS essay is for bookmen only : others will not understand. Those who crave what Keats called " a life of sensation rather than a life of thought " may pass by on the other side ; and those again who are with Walt Whitman in his " barbaric yawp " against " books distilled from books" must turn the other way unless they would risk offence. These preliminaries are for warning, not excuse.

Your good bookmen and the printed pages of their hearts' desire stand in no need of apology— or defence: defence least of all. Indeed, to be frank and at the same time to drop the mock disguise of the third person, we bookfolk, as a self-centred and self-sufficient class, would defend ourselves against defence more cheerfully and more willingly than against any other interference. We are that sort of folk—we neither advocate ourselves nor encourage the advocacy of others. We have nothing whatever to do with " movements," least of all with movements for the encouragement of

165

reading or the propagation of knowledge. We know we are a minority and will always be a minority, and we are content with our destiny : we rather like it. This may be self-protection, for there are not enough first editions to go round as it is, and as for first folio Shakespeares—those Stradivarii of books—they have passed beyond our ken since millionaire pretenders to bibliophilia have taken to hoarding them merely because they are scarce and costly. For this and other reasons we ignore fashions in books : that is to say, in old books ; the only tolerable bookish fashions are those which concern themselves with what is new. We encourage those for very selfishness. We throw new books to the Philistine wolves to divert their attention from the old—and from us.

For us the only books that are new are those that never grow old. Every age has produced a few of them, and a few are still being produced by succeeding ages. But mere production does not affect us; no bibliophile, not even the greatest, has plumbed the depths of the Pacific Ocean of books. Difficulties of production leave us unmoved. Our content is born of certainty of the riches of the untrawled deeps and still lagoons of antiquity, and

166

our faith is fortified by the instinct for hidden treasure in unlikely places—for it may be said of books more surely than of men that adversity doth acquaint them with strange bedfellows. The knight-errantry of bookmen concerns itself with the rescue of fair volumes from incompatible surroundings and hapless companionships. There is a Providence that watcheth over books thus fallen from their high estate, and every bookman of spirit can recount in proper company and on suitable occasion the hairbreadth escapes of *editiones principes*, the perilous adventures of Elzevirs, or the astounding circumstances attending the restoration of kingly Black Letters or noble Aldines ; the happy endings of all such adventures and stories being possession by the Sir Galahad of the bookman's round table. Each man seeks the Holy Grail in his own way, even in these days of obscured gleam and half-convinced effort, but few more devoutly or completely than your true Knight of the Book, who is ever ready and willing to grasp the sword Excalibur in the sacred cause. . . . Alas, I become rhetorical, which is unpardonable and misleading ; only lost causes need the administration of purple patches.

Good bookmen, however, with all their indefinable love of first editions and *rariora*, must be
carefully distinguished from those degenerate
bibliomaniacs who are merely mad on books ;
those quaint fellows who hug and hoard indis-
criminately anything printed and bound, from
tattered *incunabula* to frowsy copies of early arith-
metic, and even such ephemeral trash as old railway guides, not to forget the tabid stuff found
among the *facetiae* of the booksellers' catalogues.
These are not bookmen ; they are " collectors "—
bibliographical dustmen. The bookman is a lover
of books first and a collector afterwards. Mad he is
also, after the manner of lovers; but, after the
manner of rare lovers, he loves only what is lovely
or what reveals the inner self of him to himself—he
loves greatly and intimately. His *petite bibliothèque*,
for no true bookman wants a vast library, ap-
proximates to himself. Individually, to be sure, it
assembles more adored ones than would be
permissible or practicable in Islam, where marital
bliss is reckoned by numerical strength ; but we
bookmen love our treasures collectively, regardless
of individual intimacies. Appearances may be
against us, but, bibliographically speaking, we are

monogamous, with a difference—we embrace the one in the many. Let me confess at once that my simile is lame, and quite incapable of mounting the stile of your logic, but the pure of heart will see and understand . . . and, even then, does the most ardent and abstemious lover love more than love—" all the love of all the world in the heart of a girl "—or a man, according to sex ? But book-love is our subject.

Books are to the bookman—but what are they not ? There are, to be sure, more insistent necessities, God forgive them ; but the most convinced anchorite only achieves greater abnegation in the pursuit of his ideal because it is less attainable. We bookmen would go one better were it necessary. We would be of stout heart on bread and water—and books. We would even live in a cave, only caves are not good for calf bindings, and Russia and crushed Levant lose their virtue in low temperatures. And yet we are cave dwellers of sorts, we make about ourselves caves of books wherein we read and dream, which is our method of watching and praying, as ecstatically as any " sleepless Eremite." We live in a play of dreams and ideas prompted by masterpieces. Taunt us

169

with its artificiality, and we smile ; say that it is second-hand, life by proxy, second-fiddling to the brains of others, and we are indifferent ; hint that it is unreal—and we pity you. What is reality ?

Beside the waters of oblivion there is a fair place where storied silence breaks only to half-heard, familiar, but always new and strange communions. It is a sound heard almost without hearing, like the lisping of lake-waves or the remonstrance of some coy stream at the overtures of the young wind when the morning or the evening stars sing together. It is the sound of all sounds the most companionable : it is the whispering of the pages of books. You, if it be really you, have heard it in the quietness of your room, and you have been comforted, or, maybe, in the wizard silence of the Bodleian, where it has gone up to the painted beams as incense, incense of sound, the book-homage of ages to the God of the Printed Word who is so much mightier than the God of Battles—unless they be battles of books. Most pleasant and most comfortable of sounds, recalling the happy bookman from his eternity of words to the time that passeth, without requiring his attendance upon temporal affairs.

What is reality ? Many will answer : those
temporal affairs towards which the bookman is
recalled very properly by the fluttering pages. As
a bookman I should repudiate the many with
learned extracts, but that is the manner only of
the bookman of popular illusion. The bookman
of fact prefers to let the many have their own
temporal opinion—so long as they leave him his
books.

THE USES OF BOOKS

THE other day I was in a house where there were many books, and the people of the house spoke with such passionate affection of their bibliographical possessions that in my simplicity I imagined they were deep and untiring readers, loving the volumes not alone for their own sakes, but for the wisdom or artistry of their contents. That was the impression they desired to make, and that was the impression they did make. And whilst they prattled I handled volume after volume, browsing among the shelves with that indolent delight known to all bookish people ; but I was surprised to find—it came upon me suddenly—that the majority of the books were almost entirely unread. Most of them still possessed the familiar crackling newness, that shop-bloom which indicates the unenjoyed, the untasted state, for a book, unlike a person, gathers charm as it loses bloom : a book must be soiled to be virtuous. . . .

I have no objection to people possessing books

which they do not read : I possess books myself which I have not read, which I never intend to read, but which I would not exchange for any of those numerous volumes I " ought " to read. At the same time I am not prejudiced against those who use books as substitutes for erudition. Books at best make fickle allies in such adventures, for, no matter how loyal they may seem, they have a perilous habit of letting you down before their true friends.

It is better and safer, if you desire to impress, to use books frankly as furniture. What more engaging " finish " to a room than a portly case of well-bound " library sets "—a " run " of Walter Scott in blue calf, some Shakespeare and Dickens and George Eliot in not too tarnished coats ? And you can always win a reputation for wit and importance by saying, "Books, yes, I have them because they look nice—no time to read, these days ! "—no one will believe you, but everyone will be amused. I knew a wealthy baronet who went one better than this. His house was in the most oppressively luxurious corner of the West End, and knowing something of his open-air tastes and habits I did not expect to find books there, but to my delight I found in one of the rooms rows of curving bookshelves, filled with noble-looking tomes "rich with tarnished gold." Instinctively, I walked towards them, silently appreciative. One should always encourage the rich to improve their minds. But disappointment met me on the very threshold, for when I attempted to handle a handsomely bound copy of the *Letters of Cicero*, in green calf, *gilt extra*, with daintily inlaid red label, the whole shelf moved towards me. For a moment I felt on the edge of calamity. I had a swift vision of myself in an undignified attitude on the floor beneath a heap of literary and historical classics, plus a broken bookcase, and possibly a broken head. But fear speedily gave place to amazement. I realized at one and the same time that the bookcase was an imposing and delightful fraud—it was nothing more than a cupboard door on whose face were glued the backs of make-believe books resting securely upon imitation shelves. My attempt to detach Cicero had caused the door to open, and as my scattered wits returned to work I learned the secret of what lay behind this veneer of books. It was first revealed by a fragrance, luxurious and familiar, for

the semblance of classical lore screened a nest of
shelves closely packed with boxes of cigars ! With
due and fitting reverence I closed the door and,
like Bruce of Scotland, flung myself down (in an
easy chair, of course) to think.

Now what more dainty compliment, I thought,
could be paid to books than that ingenious fraud
behind me ? Here was a man who was evidently
a past master of the gentle English art of compromise, a man who, you may be sure, knew how
to make good terms with earth and heaven.
Books he knew to be good things, but for himself
he had no use for them. Still, they were good,
imposing, and, doubtless, ennobling ; had not
good men of all the nations down all the ages said
so ? Therefore, he had argued, let us do homage
where homage is due and, incidentally, keep up
appearances. Having no use for books, he made
the best of his respect for those who had. Further-
more, he did so in a practical way, worthy of a man
of spirit, who moved in the " best " circles, by
decorating the receptacles of more useful things—
cigars for instance—with imitation bibliographical
treasures. He erected monuments of books before
the shrine of the Goddess Nicotine. And despite

175

the subterfuge I am not sure that he was not making as worthy a use of books as many whose pretensions approach more nearly to reality. But, at the same time, it would have been less gracious, but more strictly in keeping with the tradition of honesty, if he had kept real books on his shelves and consumed them as cigar lighters. The latter method of dealing with books would confer a double blessing upon men, in the first instance by getting rid of a lot of unnecessary old books, and in the second by providing additional royalties for the authors of new ones. And the Goddess Nicotine, one might imagine, would be more readily propitiated by the gift of fire : as the Muses, with their traditional incense.

Books are curious and elusive things, and, after all, no man can say with any degree of certainty for what purpose they may be used to the best advantage. Some people use them for propping up decrepit furniture, a practice that will commend itself to the practical and the haphazard alike; others use them as missiles. William Morris hurled a fifteenth century quarto, which he would allow no one to touch but himself, at the head of a person who had irritated him. Throwing *incunabula* at tiresome

folk has much to be said for it; but the uses of books
are by no means exhausted by such passionate acts.

All manner and conditions of folks use books for
all kinds and conditions of purposes. Some sell
them for money, just as others publish, and others
again write them, or review them, for the same
reason ; some, as we have seen, use them as
furniture ; others put them on the tops of piano-
fortes ; others again collect them as men collect
postage stamps, old coins, or dead butterflies ;
others lend them, and, as a matter of course, there
are those who borrow them ; others steal them ;
many beg them, particularly from authors (this is
a growing class and ought to be dealt with under
the Vagrancy Acts) ; some use them as presents,
or distribute them as prizes ; quite a considerable
minority of the population buy them, and I can
vouch for it as a fact that some few actually read
them, though in all fairness I must say there are
not so many of these last. It will thus be seen that
books are not nearly so useless as many very
excellent people imagine them to be ; in fact, they
are used for innumerable purposes, many more,
indeed, than I have set forth or have space to
announce : and even were I to enumerate all

within my ken my ingenious reader would be
able to suggest more, for the uses of books are
as varied as life, and as infinite.

I also have my special other than studious uses
for books. By books I mean those printed and
bound pages which have no other object than to
be books. Some even of the above uses are also
mine, but I am now writing of my special and
peculiar use of those books that are content to be
merely books and nothing more. There are
volumes got up to look like books, but which
come, properly speaking, in the category of tools
—school books, technical books, primers, theo-
logical books, treatises, glossaries, concordances,
and gazetteers.[1] Needless to say that when I write

[1] Charles Lamb called such books *biblia a-biblia;* but he
included in this class books which other bookmen would class as
veritable *biblia :* " In this catalogue of *books which are no books—
biblia a-biblia* "—he said, " I reckon Court Calendars, Direc-
tories, Pocket Books (the literary excepted), Draught Boards,
bound and lettered at the back, Scientific Treatises, Almanacs,
Statutes at large ; the works of Hume, Gibbon, Robertson,
Beattie, Soame Jenyns, and, generally, all those volumes which
' no gentleman's library should be without ' : the Histories of
Flavius Josephus (that learned Jew), and Paley's *Moral Philosophy.* With these exceptions, I can read almost anything.
I bless my stars for a taste so catholic, so unexcluding." " De-
tached Thoughts on Books and Reading "—*The Last Essays of
Elia,* p. 38. Temple Library edition.

of books I am no more alluding to these than I am alluding to picks or plough-shares. Nor should you conclude that I am deprecating them. If what I have written gives you such an idea, pray forgive me ; my intention is to define rather than to condemn, for from the point of view of practical utility the tool-book must always take precedence. Still, no real bookman would ever dream of collecting that type of book, any more than he would dream of accumulating rows of Bradshaw or Debrett or the *Almanach de Gotha*. Such treasures are for use, not collection, they are part of the equipment of those who take travel and the upper classes seriously. They are necessities, and, to adapt a famous saying, I care not who has the necessary books so long as I have the bookish luxuries.

At the same time it must not be forgotten that there are instances in the history of tool-books in which certain favoured specimens, by some happy arrangement of circumstances, have achieved immortality. Such are Izaak Walton's *Compleat Angler*, White's *Natural History of Selborne*, Burton's *Anatomy of Melancholy*, Bunyan's *Pilgrim's Progress*, Jeremy Taylor's *Sermons*, Culpeper's *Herbal*, and Sir Thomas Browne's *Urn Burial*.

Books of this type are reserved for our warmest affection. They are not books from which one has sought to learn anything, they are books which have caused one to experience something ; that is why your true book-lover never wants to part with them. You may never read again the books you really love, but you are none the less never quite happy when you are away from them. You may promise yourself a second reading, but the years slip by and the promise is still unfulfilled, it is still a promise, a promise raised to immortality, because in itself it is the confession of an experience, requiring no further fulfilment.

The fact that you promise to read a book again means nothing more than that the book in question has given you joy, been to you an experience, an adventure ; your promise to read it again is your thanks, your homage, your benediction. That is small enough reward for so great a boon, but mortal man can do no more. The great books are those that have opened magic casements, and once they have done that they have attained their end. It is not only books that do this—any other work of art may do it just as well, and certain rare experiences in life can do it even better; but a book

180

is the readiest key to the mysteries—and the most friendly. It takes you gently by the hand, as it were, and so long as you are willing leads you into the light.

But my chief use for books is just to have them about me, not merely for reference, but for—well, when I come to think of it, I cannot quite say. There is probably no sufficient reason, although had I space I might invent many. Books for me are mysterious urns full of the wonder and joy of life, full of tragic thought and light suggestion. Books suggest more than they tell ; and they tell more than they suggest, according to the way you look at them and the mood of the moment. For, after all, it takes two to make a book, an author and a reader. The former initiates a thought or a view of a thought, and puts his impressions into words, but the matter does not end there, it ends only when he has found someone who will be the receptacle of that thought, who will complete the magic circle of communion.

No book is complete until it has been appreciated, and a great reader is as rare as a great writer : a great reader may be far more unique. We have records of our great writers, but only a

181

few of our great readers are known. There are many extensive readers, but extensive reading is not the same thing ; nor has great reading any necessary connection with scholarship or learning. To read well is to read with insight and sympathy, to become one with your author, to let him live through you, adding what he is to what you are without losing your own identity. Verily, to write books is easier than to read them as they should be read.

The value of reading lies in the opportunity it gives us of being able to discover what we are and what we think, as well as what others are and what others think. It needs the faculty of comparison and a sharp instrument of thought. Reading is also the most pleasant way of doing nothing, of resting, a fine art in a hustling world.

The dearth of great readers, however, may explain the curiously varied attitude adopted towards books in our age, but it ought to help us towards a philosophic forbearance of any bookishness which may appear strange or unwise. You see, books nowadays are articles of commerce ; they must be printed because people want to make money out of them, and they must be sold for the same reason.

Therefore we all possess books in varying quantities, but most of us put them to every imaginable use except that for which they were made.

So perhaps after all the most reverent of attitudes towards books was that adopted by my wealthy baronet. He at least knew where he was, and created a respectable illusion of bookishness which was dissipated but not destroyed every time he went to the cupboard for a cigar. To him a book was merely a symbol of life ; a cigar was life itself. Which of us dare say he was wrong ?

OF CHEERFUL BOOKS

I AM an unabashed reader of books : all kinds
of books—good books and bad books, well-
written and ill-written ; books with a purpose,
and books whose existence only the nicest
sophistry could justify ; books created by genius,
and books built by talent standing on its head to
attract attention ; I even read books made to sell.
I can and do read at all times and in all places—
standing up, and sitting or lying down ; in chair or
bed ; on trains or 'buses or boats ; in houses,
gardens, theatres (when the play is dull) ; at
concerts (reading to music is a discovery and not
nearly so offensive to the musicians as talking to
music) ; at meals (this is a delight which deserves
an essay to itself)—in short, it would not be easy to
name time or place or season which I should find
inappropriate to the indulgence of this habit ; and
yet with all its catholicity and its complete
indifference for the feelings of others, I can say
with that self-satisfaction which comes only to
those who admit being addicted to at least one

habit which is no use to anyone but themselves
that I could never bring myself to anything
approaching enjoyment of an intentionally cheerful book. Cheerful books, or shall I say " cheery "
books, make me sad : professional optimism
reduces me to ashes.

Let me state also, lest there should be any mis-
take, that I am pleased with my weakness, and far
from being in an apologetic mood am inclined to
be lofty about it. I think cheery books are a snare
and a pitfall, and cheery writers people with
sinister designs upon our purses and our brains.
They pamper a degenerate mood : they buttress
melancholy instead of destroying it. All the worst
literature and the worst art of modern times are
the result of a demand for cheerfulness—a demand
which has its roots deep down in moral cowardice.
The demand that art should be the toy of our idle
moments has produced the shoddy art of commerce, all the trivial burlesques and farces, all the
" light " operas and novels with happy endings,
all the tinsel and the shallow thought and pale
emotion, the sickening " heart interest," which
serve the more starved of our faculties for mental
and imaginative recreation. In such an age as

ours, when haste and insecurity have robbed us of half the joy of life, an easily assimilated art is necessary, but that is no excuse for bad art ; and the need of inspiration such as books can give and the joy thereof is so real that the subject is worth further consideration.

Cheerfulness, as a matter of fact, is often a characteristic of great literature ; but that cheerfulness is not the superficial and trivial thing usually associated with the demand for " happy endings " and the like. It springs rather from the deeps of spiritual courage and imaginative honesty, and it has little to do with either an optimistic or a pessimistic view of life. I might even go so far as to say that courage before life, no matter whether one has to face a danger, an unpleasant fact, or a new idea, is always cheering, or, what is better still, inspiring. For, in spite of the fact that it is always good to be cheerful, the constant demand that artists and writers and composers should devote their energies and genius to " cheering you up " is smug and cowardly, and destructive of all the best art work. If there be a common denominator in the present age it is the universal desire to be " cheered up." Such a

186

mental state reflects seriously upon the age and ourselves, who are trustees and wardens for the future, for it means, if it mean anything at all, that we are devoid of that inner richness which is the only true happiness, and, in the last resort, the only true life. A healthy being should be able to keep himself cheerful, just as he keeps, or is supposed to keep, himself healthy. Only invalids require doctors ; it is not the business of art or literature to prescribe for sick souls and depressed spirits. Art galleries and libraries should be looked upon as temples rather than hospitals. And so we should not demand only of a book that it minister to a melancholy mood due to wrong social habits. Such a practice is like alleviating pain by means of an opiate, instead of removing the cause of pain ; or like the defeatist habit of erecting staring washable buildings instead of cleansing the smoke-defiled air of our cities. The demand for cheerfulness in art is one with these.

But I imagine that all people worth a moment's consideration who desire what is cheering in literature desire also what is inspiring. The test of great literature is its power of inspiring the reader with some of the inspiration which went to the

187

making of the book. We are in the habit of talking of inspired books as if these were confined to the volumes which contain the expression of religious thought. But all real books are inspired : all great literature is essentially religious in attitude and outlook. And in the last resort in certain ages, such, I think, as our own, it is not the business of books to cheer us and comfort us : it is the business of books to inspire us with a desire for a fuller life, to environ us with wonder and delight at great human achievement, and still greater human achievement to come, and to strengthen our personal insight and courage by showing us what we are and what we might be. Books that serve such a purpose are cheering books in the only admissible sense.

If you will think about the books which have come your way you will find that they fall roughly into two classes : books that exhilarate and books that depress—books that awaken the soul and books that send the soul to sleep. There is, of course, a place for each, but we require more of those of the first class. We require rosemary for remembrance rather than poppies for oblivion. We are not sufficiently awake to the wonders and possibilities of the day, and yet, as Thoreau said, " there is more day to dawn." But the position is not so much that we have to choose between books that exhilarate and books that depress, as between certain definite cheering qualities in books. If you are cheered on to still finer and finer actions by what you read ; if your chosen books add something to your consciousness and personal power, then you may say you have chosen well. As to the other books we need not worry—they are not our concern. The great cheering of great books is there for all who desire it. Those who don't may take their ease with the demi-geniuses, dipping lightly into shallow basins of thought and bathing their temples with the tepid waters of the circulating library novel. They have the right to compose their leisure in their own way. If they like their reading to be as insubstantial as puffing a cigarette or toying with a liqueur, that is their own business. It cheers them up. But to make no further demands of literature is to kill literature.

ON READING ALOUD

I N the first place you should not read anything
merely because it is popular or readable—or,
above all, because other people have read it—
more especially if it has been read or recited by a
great actor. You would thus pass the *Christmas
Carol* in compliment to Sir Squire Bancroft, and
you would permit *The Dream of Eugene Aram* to
rest upon the laurels won for it by Sir Henry
Irving. Such masterpieces and their like must ever
be on the *index expurgatorius* of the reading aloud
I have in mind. They have become too loud to be
heard.

On the same principle *Gunga Din* and *Mandalay*
are anathema. The reader should abstain from
Kipling as he would the plague. This is no
reflection upon eminent writers who have had the
misfortune to become popular at Bohemian Concerts and Penny Readings. They will always have
honour done to them at such admirable functions,
but in the reading aloud of my dreams they would
be as matter out of place—what Walter Pater

would have called "otiose." Nor is it that such works have become too obvious—only dull people fear the obvious—it is not easy to explain why they are forbidden, perhaps they have been spoiled by elocution. Which brings me to my second point.

Elocution is fatal to reading aloud—as fatal almost as an audience—and this is my third and final negation. You must above all things abstain from audiences in the popularly accepted sense. Good reading and crowds go not together. They cancel and obliterate one another. Melodrama is for the crowd; melodrama and humour; senti-mentality is for the crowd—these postulate emotional excess and require the oracular and hyperbolic arts. They require play-acting and elocution. Reading aloud requires neither. It is the art of elocution born again, and born different; it is more intimate, more subtle, and more per-sonal. It regards broad effects as improper.

There are some that will murmur against the severity of these restrictions. Such criticism is courted and anticipated; my restrictions are meant to be severe—but not crippling. They impose limitations deliberately that freedom may survive for a definite and clearly visioned end—an

191

end in itself rather than a device for passing the time. That end is an extension of reading from oneself so that another or a few others, kindred in taste, should participate in the experience.

A certain formality is imposed by any reading aloud, but in any fine or discriminating reading of the kind the process leading up to it is free and natural—the culmination of a persistent inclination. Every real lover of good writing is moved on the instant of discovery to communicate his experience in sympathetic hearing. For although the reading of books is the most satisfying of all solitary experiences, books in themselves being the best of companions, such companionship in silence and solitude is not always desirable. Fine reading is not more miserly than fine friendship. The impulse to share what is good with one's kind is, however, deep-rooted.

You can, of course, lend books, but that is not the same thing; besides, there are objections to lending books, even to your best friends. If you happen to be a bookman as well as a bibliophile of spirit you mistrust book-borrowers, not alone because experience or rumour may have taught you that in every borrower of books lurks a biblioclept, but because of an indefinable jealousy of all caresses save your own, particularly out of your sight. Who can say what unseemly familiarities may be pressed upon your endeared tomes if you are not by? What slights, perchance, or what neglects? No proper bookman will expose his treasures to such risks. But, believe me, his chariness is not parsimony; no niggardly instinct prompts him: it is love, pure love, as blind as any that has lit the lamp of romance, blind to everything but its enraptured self . . . but I digress. . . .

Reading aloud, in brief, should be the communication of your best reading—the sacrament of choice literary experience. The instinct which prompts it is so familiar that recapitulation is unnecessary. By Apollo! you say at the fine moment, that's a great passage. I must read it to Marius next time he is here! And there is just a hint of sadness in that he is not present at the first fine careless rapture of discovery. Every good reader is making such discoveries, if indeed good reading can be said to have any other object, and every discovery thus cries out to be shared. Marius, as we are aware, is not always at hand, and

193   N

meetings in a workaday world must, perforce, be left to chance—leaving forgetfulness at large and the high mood time to slip " into the dusk of alien things." Thus the sharing of a happy experience, one of the few things worth having in these glimpses of the moon, is like to be lost or needlessly delayed.

Those who are able to fashion themselves for reading aloud are able to conserve their best experiences and repeat them as opportunity provides. With practice they learn to note opportunity and to take it, for reading aloud cannot be indulged at will : it must either happen naturally, like art in Whistler's phrase, or occur by arrangement. Indeed it is an art, the art of combining time and people and subject in one harmonious communion. That is—at its best ; but one does not always achieve the best, one aims above the mark to hit the mark. Nor would I encourage the idea that reading aloud is in itself exalted ; on the contrary, it is familiar and friendly and capable of infinite variation to suit all tastes. Wherever two or three people are gathered together there is your temple of the muses—tastes being equal. Observe that equality of taste is the sole indispensable to the practice, always bearing in mind my initial restrictions. A good voice and an easy, expressive manner are supplementary advantages making for success, and if the one is a gift the other is an accomplishment, and may with perseverance be attained—but blessed be he that possesseth each, and twice blessed them that hear him.

Finally, read only what interests you. Good taste has no golden rules—but it is oftenest found in those who please themselves. By a mysterious alchemy of the soul those who please themselves infect others with their happiness and attract them to its causes.

But sharing the joy of reading is not the sole aim of reading aloud. The practice intensifies reading and varies it. Some German curmudgeon of a philosopher has put up the bogey that reading is dangerous because it is thinking with someone else's brain. That is very German, and very silly. Great thinkers have invariably been great readers. Great poets always drop their buckets into the wells of brother bards. Shakespeare read and pilfered every book of his day. Shelley got drunk on Plato ; and " what porridge ate John Keats ? " —why, the best full-grained Chaucer and fine-cut

Spenser washed down with flagons and flagons of Shakespeare and Chapman. So let no dour German scare us out of our books.

In reading aloud you are greatly privileged, first to consort with all that is noble and beautiful in thought and imagination, and then to introduce your thinkers and dreamers to your best friends. You adventure amongst masterpieces and spread the glorious news of your discoveries and conquests. It is not easy to name news better worth spreading. But with the privilege goes a grave responsibility, for in the silence of the study you may read well or ill without harming your author, but when you read aloud you add something to him, you add your vision to his, your mind to his, your voice to his ; you become his spokesman and interpreter. Therefore, humility, friends, humility and reverence ; let no voice of brass or insolence of mind cheapen your effort or his work. Your reading must reflect his meaning, and for the time being your voice must be modulated to the pitch of his, or what he fain would have had his voice could it have been attuned to the mellow notes of the written word; and here at length my argument is set forth, its virtue, if it have any, stands revealed, its pitfalls indicated. But if the clue of intimacy be sedulously followed these last may be avoided. Venture only upon the little master-pieces and avoid the heroic. Be urbane even in your lyric moods, remembering always that grand passions are silent and that manners and character are talkative. Let your reading aloud be good talk.